The **Sewing Machine**
Accessory Bible

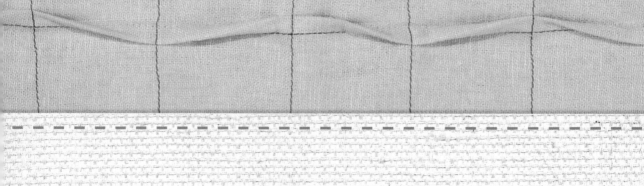

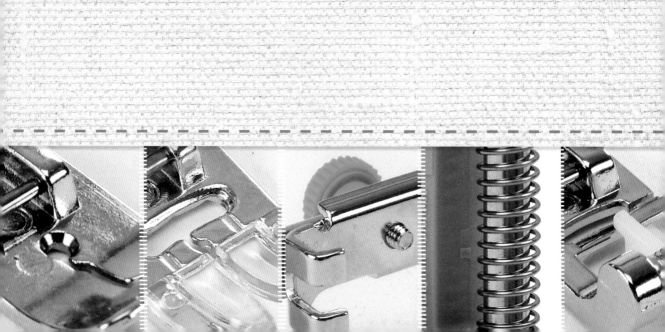

The Sewing Machine
Accessory Bible

WENDY GARDINER & LORNA KNIGHT

www.stmartins.com

ST. MARTIN'S GRIFFIN
175 Fifth Avenue, New York, N.Y. 10010
Distributed in Canada by H. B. Fenn and Company, Ltd
PRINTED IN CHINA

Library of Congress Cataloging-in-Publication
Data available upon request.

ISBN: 978-0-312-67658-2

QUAR.SMAB

Conceived, designed, and produced by
Quarto Publishing plc
The Old Brewery
6 Blundell Street
London N7 9BH

Project Editor: Chloe Todd Fordham
Art Editor: Emma Clayton
Designer: Karin Skånberg
Picture Researcher: Sarah Bell
Photographer: Phil Wilkins
Illustrator: Kuo Kang Chen
Art Director: Caroline Guest
Creative Director: Moira Clinch
Publisher: Paul Carslake

Color separation in Singapore by
PICA Digital Pte Ltd
Printed in China by
1010 Printing International Ltd

First U.S. Edition: April 2011

10 9 8 7 6 5 4 3 2 1

Contents

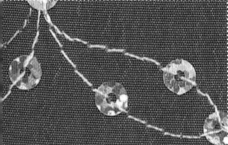

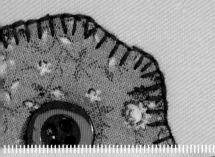

Authors' foreword

We love our sewing machines, so have thoroughly enjoyed writing this book and playing with the many sewing gadgets available. All sewing machines come with a selection of presser feet, and there are so many other specialist feet and gadgets available, designed to make sewing easier. However, it is not always obvious what these strange-looking feet are for. Dip into this book and soon you will know and be itching to have a go!

Best of all, you don't have to have a top-of-the-range model to use all these wonderful sewing aids—lots of these glorious feet can be used on even the most basic machines. Also, they are not just all about specialist techniques—many of these feet help to perform basic sewing techniques or simply feed the fabric evenly and smoothly as you sew.

This is a deli sandwich of a book. The outer wrapping is all about getting the most from your sewing machine and includes our choice of essential sewing kit, a clear guide to the anatomy of a sewing machine, a comprehensive guide to needle, thread, and fabric choices, as well as buying advice for choosing sewing machines, embellisher, and overlockers. In addition, there is a very handy section on troubleshooting tips so you know what to do when things go wrong.

The delicious filling comprises a healthy mix of getting the best from basic feet and having fun with the more exotic ones. We've shown what each foot is, and a step-by-step sequence of how it works, together with a series of suggestions in the "Ideas Files" so you can experiment yourself.

This book is all about having fun with your machine, tackling any project you want with confidence, and being assured of some truly creative results. We hope you enjoy dipping into it as much as we have enjoyed writing it.

Happy sewing!

Wendy Gardiner and Lorna Knight

About this book

At the heart of this book are sewing machine feet. Four colorful chapters take you through over 25 "must-have" feet attachments for the beginner or experienced sewer—as selected by experienced authors, Wendy and Lorna.

THE FEET

The feet are organized logically into groups by either sewing technique or ease of use. Chapter two is devoted to basic feet that come with nearly all machines, such as the zigzag foot, zipper foot, and buttonhole foot. In chapter three, you will discover feet to help you with difficult-to-sew fabrics such as leather or chiffons. If it's edges you want to sew, look no further than chapter four, and if you're keen to add beads or ribbons without the fuss of hand sewing, you will find what you're looking for in chapter five.

Every foot is explained in full. Easy-to-follow step-by-step instructions demonstrate how to use the attachment for best results, and a creative "Ideas File" showcases a few other effects, so that you can truly see what the foot is capable of. There's a picture of two sample pages below, so you can see what you're getting.

MACHINES AND OTHER ACCESSORIES

If you're picking up this book, the chances are you already have a sewing machine—or at least you're thinking of buying one or upgrading. The book begins with outlining "Essential kit," so that you're armed to set up and sew, and finishes with a "Buyer's guide" containing advice on basic, mid-range, and top-end machines, what to look for, and which one will suit you. Everything you need to get going—and to keep sewing.

Feet can be difficult to distinguish and brands may vary, but with these photographic references, you will know exactly what you're looking for when you visit your nearest suppliers.

Extensive "Ideas Files" show the full potential of the foot and will get you sewing creatively.

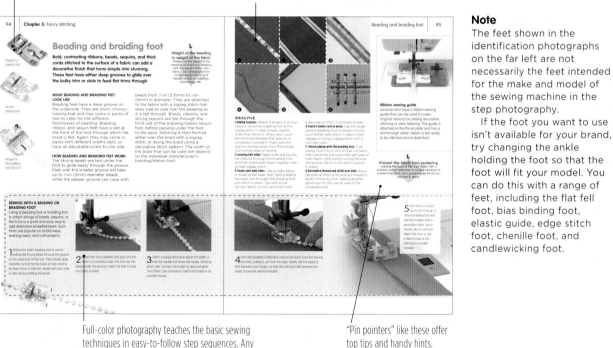

Note

The feet shown in the identification photographs on the far left are not necessarily the feet intended for the make and model of the sewing machine in the step photography.

If the foot you want to use isn't available for your brand, try changing the ankle holding the foot so that the foot will fit your model. You can do this with a range of feet, including the flat fell foot, bias binding foot, elastic guide, edge stitch foot, chenille foot, and candlewicking foot.

Full-color photography teaches the basic sewing techniques in easy-to-follow step sequences. Any difficult stitching is reiterated in a detailed close-up, helping you to achieve professional results.

"Pin pointers" like these offer top tips and handy hints.

CHAPTER 1
Essential kit

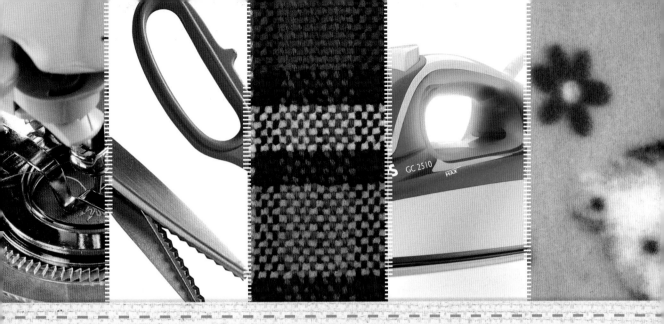

Let's begin at the beginning! Before starting any sewing project, you need some essential supplies, ranging from haberdashery to a sewing machine, needles, threads, and fabrics. In this chapter we list what we think are the must-have items as well as demystifying the sewing machine so that you can confidently get it out of the box or cupboard and sew away with confidence. We've also provided a low-down on thread choice, needles, and a comprehensive guide to fabrics. By the end of the chapter, you'll be armed with all the knowledge you need to set up and sew!

Anatomy of a sewing machine

All sewing machines have the basic components in the same place and although they differ greatly in functions and facilities (depending on the type and price of the machine), it is comforting to know that the basics are always the same.

Many sewing machines are self-lubricating nowadays, so you don't need to oil them (although they do still need maintenance) and most will have the drop feed dogs facility, allowing you to control the direction you stitch and the length of the stitch (see pages 80–83, Darning/embroidery foot).

Here are the basic components that make up the anatomy of a sewing machine.

Needle (1): This has a flat back on the shank which fits into the needle holder, flat to back (check the user's manual). Tighten the needle by hand and then with the supplied screwdriver so that it cannot work loose when stitching. The needle position can be altered on most machines, from left, center to right, and variations in between on more expensive machines. This enables you to stitch close to the fabric edge, at a regular $5/8$in (1.5cm) away, or further left to provide a wider seam allowance.

Throat plate (2): Usually made of metal, this has holes through which the feed dogs move, as well as a hole for the needle. It will also have markings to the right of the needle, showing different spacing from the default needle position to create specific seam allowances.

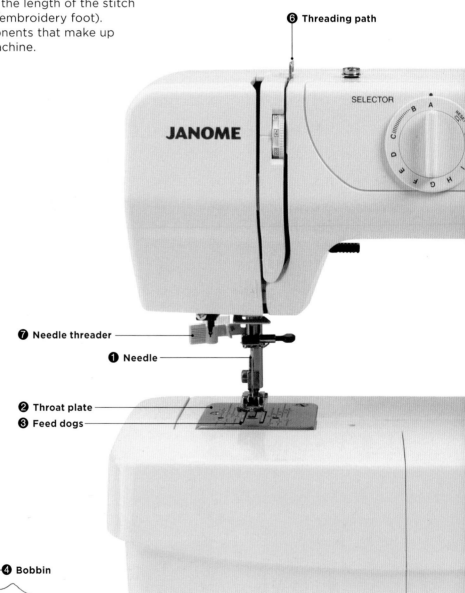

❻ Threading path

SELECTOR

JANOME

❼ Needle threader

❶ Needle

❷ Throat plate

❸ Feed dogs

❹ Bobbin

Feed dogs (3): These are the jagged gripper teeth that come up through the throat plate to help move the fabric through the machine as you sew. They work in conjunction with the presser foot. Most machines now have a facility to drop the feed dogs, which means they are lowered and stay below the throat plate so do not guide the fabric at all. This is useful if you wish to decide the direction you stitch (see pages 80–83, Darning/embroidery foot).

Bobbin cover: On sewing machines with drop-in bobbins, this is usually a clear plastic cover that forms part of the throat plate. Generally, it has a printed guide that shows you how to thread the bobbin once it is dropped in place. On front-loading machines, the bobbin case is part of the body of the machine, which opens up to reveal the bobbin holder.

Bobbin (4): The bobbin thread links with the top thread to form the stitches when the needle comes down through the throat plate. The bobbin thread forms the underside of the stitching. Top-loading/drop-in bobbins are easy to insert, by simply dropping in place and laying the thread through the tension, as shown on the bobbin cover. Front-loading bobbins sit inside a metal case, which is then inserted into the body of the machine at the front. It is important to ensure that the shaped case (which has a protruding arm) is inserted into its slot correctly so that it doesn't work itself loose. Make sure you insert the bobbin the right way round, as it can cause skipped stitches or broken thread if it is not inserted correctly.

Bobbin winding (5): Usually located on the top of the machine, the bobbin is placed on the winding spindle and thread, laid through a bobbin tension disc (following a printed path). The bobbin spindle may then need to be moved toward the winder, which in turn disengages the sewing mechanism and needle while winding the bobbin. Most bobbins will stop automatically when they are full. **Note:** On basic models, you may need to disengage the needle before bobbin winding by pulling out part of the balance wheel.

Threading path (6): There is usually a clearly printed and numbered path to follow when threading the top thread. First, the thread spool is put on the spindle and then kept in place with a thread retainer disc (this prevents the reel from bouncing up and down the spindle, which in turn prevents threads tangling and snapping). The **thread spindle** may be upright or lie horizontally. The thread will then go through a loop or hook, down and up through the tension discs, through a loop attached to the needle lift/lowering mechanism before going through the needle. **Note:** It is important that the presser foot is raised when threading the machine, as this releases the tension discs and ensures the thread will lie between them easily.

A second thread spindle is often supplied in the tools, which is useful for twin needle stitching when you use two top threads. (If you don't have a separate spindle for the second thread, just wind two bobbins and stack them on one spindle.)

Thread cutter: Most machines have a handily placed thread cutter on the left side of the machine or behind the needle. This enables you to cut the thread tails evenly and leave enough to start the next row of stitching without the needle unthreading itself. Many of the more expensive models also have automatic thread cutters, accessed by the touch of a button.

Needle threader (7): Many new sewing machines have an auto needle threader to help thread the eye of the needle quickly and easily. This may be operated with the touch of a button or by lowering a lever. If your machine doesn't have one, hold a small scrap of white paper behind the needle eye

Thread spindle 6

5 Bobbin winding

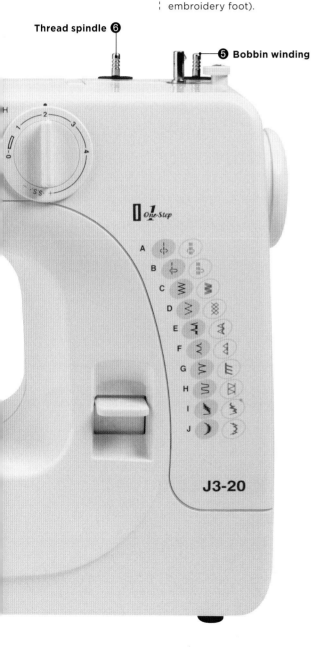

One-Step

J3-20

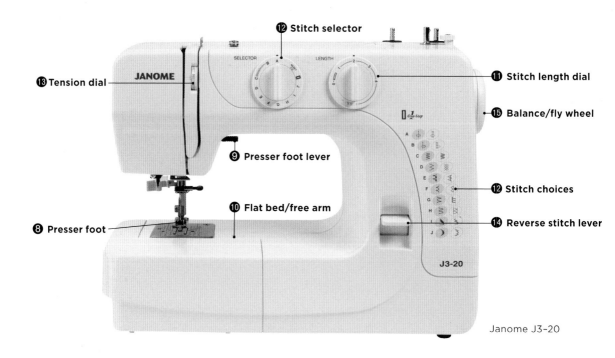

⑫ Stitch selector

⑬ Tension dial

JANOME

⑪ Stitch length dial

⑮ Balance/fly wheel

⑨ Presser foot lever

⑫ Stitch choices

⑩ Flat bed/free arm

⑭ Reverse stitch lever

⑧ Presser foot

J3-20

Janome J3-20

when threading as it helps to make the eye more visible.

Presser foot (8): The presser foot holds the fabric flat and helps to feed it through as you stitch. Most are snap-on or clip-on, making them easy to remove and replace. Bernina models have a shank attached to the presser foot, which is inserted onto a holder. Lots of different presser feet are available in varying shapes and indentations to help with different sewing techniques.

Presser foot lever (9): This is accessed through the sewing area and to the back of the tension/thread path. The lever is raised to raise the presser foot and lowered to lower the presser foot. Always make sure it is raised when threading the machine.

Flat bed/free arm (10): The flat bed is the surface area around the needle which provides a flat surface on which to lay the fabric as it is being sewn. Many machines have the option to convert to "free arm,"

which involves removing some of the flat bed to reveal a more narrow surface area around the throat plate. When using the free arm, there is a clear space in the front, back, and under the sewing area, enabling you to work on circular small items such as cuffs, sleeves, and pant legs.

Stitch width dial: Stitch width dial is similar to stitch length dial. It offers the choice of stitch widths, or side-to-side length of the stitch, and is applicable to any sideways stitch, such as zigzag. It may be numbered or just have a sliding scale. The higher the number or wider the printed scale, the wider the stitch.

Stitch length dial (11): This offers the choice of stitch length from top to bottom of the stitch. It is usually numbered. The smaller the number, the smaller the stitch will be. Shorter length stitches are used on lightweight fabric. 2.5 is average stitch length for light to medium fabrics.

Longer stitch length is used for gathering, basting, or when sewing several layers of thick fabric.

Stitch choices (12): On many machines, the choice of built-in stitches is printed on the front, or on a flap that sits above the top of the machine. You make your choice by turning a dial (or by pressing a button) to select the required stitch number. On some of the more basic models, the stitches may not be numbered but there will be a window in which the stitch selected is shown.

Tension dial (13): The top tension is controlled by a dial on the front or top of the machine, usually just above the needle area. It is numbered and has the most common or default tension highlighted. Most modern machines are very forgiving and it is unusual for any adjustment to be needed for regular sewing. If you do adjust the tension, do so a little at a time. Perfect stitches are formed with the

top thread visible on the top of the fabric, and the bobbin thread visible on the underside.

Reverse stitch lever (14): Back or reverse stitching is used to firmly anchor stitching at the start and end of a seam. There will be a lever to press (often on the lower right-hand side of the front of the machine) or a button just above the needle. Levers usually have to be held down to continue stitching in reverse, and when released will revert to forward stitching.

Balance/fly wheel (15): Located on the right-hand side of the machine, turning the balance wheel lowers and raises the needle one step at a time. This is useful when checking that the needle won't hit the side of the presser foot or throat plate when you want to take just one stitch. On older models, an inner part of the wheel may be pushed in or pulled out to disengage the needle for bobbin winding.

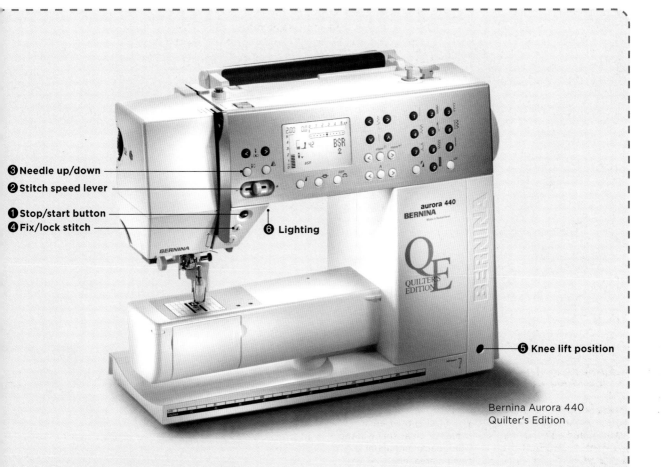

③ Needle up/down
② Stitch speed lever
① Stop/start button
④ Fix/lock stitch
⑥ Lighting
⑤ Knee lift position

Bernina Aurora 440
Quilter's Edition

EXTRA FEATURES FOUND ON MID-RANGE TO TOP-END COMPUTERIZED MACHINES

Stop/start button (1): Can be used instead of the foot pedal (which usually has to be unplugged from the machine). It is an ideal feature for disabled or infirm people who have difficulty using a foot pedal or when you wish to stitch long seams, for instance. It is a good idea to test this function on fabric scraps as it often makes the machine stitch very quickly. Alter the speed by adjusting the stitch speed dial.

Stitch speed lever (2): Enables you to control the speed of stitching by moving the lever from fast to slow, or anywhere in

between. Once you have selected the speed you prefer, no matter how hard you press the foot pedal, the machine will maintain that speed.

Needle up/down (3): Button found just above the needle, which gives you the option of always stopping either with the needle down, or in the up position. Needle down is very useful when stitching fiddly work and you wish to keep the fabric securely anchored by the needle when raising and lowering the presser foot. It's equally useful to stop in the up position when sewing regular seams.

Fix/lock stitch (4): An alternative and neater option to reverse stitching as it means stitching on the spot, locking in the stitches. This button is usually found above the needle, together with the stop/start and needle up/down buttons.

Knee lift (5): Shaped metal rod inserted into the front of the machine, which raises and lowers the presser foot without the need to take your hands from the work. You'll need to get used to using it, but it can be a real boon if you have arthritis or sew a lot of appliqué and need to raise and lower the presser foot repeatedly.

Lighting (6): Basic machines have one internal light over the needle area, but as machines increase in complexity, so does the sewing light facility, adding a choice of light color and a greater number of lighting positions.

Foot pedal: All machines have a foot pedal, which is used to control the speed of stitching. The harder you press, the faster you stitch.

Tape measure

Must-have tools

Before starting on any sewing project, it's a good idea to have some necessary supplies to hand. We've put together our list of essential kit so that you will be ready to sew just about anything.

MEASURING AND MARKING

Tape measure: Have at least one good tape measure (and if you've had one for years, replace it as they can stretch). A retractable tape, with imperial and metric measurements, is ideal.

Point turner: Not only has this short plastic or wooden ruler got a point at one end, used to push out corners, it has approximately 4in (10cm) of markings along one edge which can be used to measure and turn up hem allowances, depth of pleats, etc.

Erasable marking pens: A wide choice is available, from those that fade away after a day or two, to those that disappear when washed. These are great for quick-and-easy markings of darts, zipper or button placement, pleats, etc., but try them on a scrap of fabric first to make sure they don't "bleed" into the fabric.

Chalk pens/wheels/blocks: Chalk is great for temporarily marking fabric as it can be brushed away once you have finished using it. Chalk comes in a variety of colors and shapes, from traditional pencils and tailor's triangles to chalk wheels. These hold fine chalk dust, released as the serrated wheel is run along the position to be marked, which is particularly useful for marking darts, pleats, etc.

CUTTING TOOLS

Dressmaking shears: Essential for all sewing, good dressmaking shears should be kept away from the family and used only to cut fabric. Shears are available for right- or left-handed use. They have bigger handles than scissors, usually with a larger hole for the thumb, and long blades to cut fabric smoothly. Shears with a fine serrated blade are ideal for cutting lightweight slippery fabric as the tiny serrations grip the fabric as it is cut.

Pinking shears: Another must-have, pinking shears have saw-tooth blades that provide the "pinked" edge. They are ideal for quickly neatening raw edges of cottons and other non-fray fabrics.

Needlework scissors: Small embroidery scissors are useful for snipping into seam allowances, clipping thread ends, curves, notches, etc. The smaller blades provide greater control when handling small areas.

Seam ripper/quick-unpick: This tool is usually part of the sewing-machine tool kit. Not only is it particularly handy for unpicking stitching, it can be used to cut open buttonholes easily. It has a sharp prong with curved blade at the base, which is the cutting surface.

Needlework scissors

Chalk pens

Chalk blocks

Don't press marking-pen marks
Never press over marks made with a marking pen as the hot iron may set them permanently.

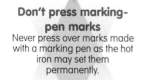

Erasable markers

Quick-unpick

Dressmaking shears

Pinking shears

PRESSING AIDS

Steam iron: This is essential when sewing. Always press sewn seams before stitching over them again to ensure a neat and professional finish. Pressing also embeds the stitches so that the seam is smooth and ripple-free. Use with a pressing cloth (a square of organza is ideal as it is transparent and withstands high temperatures).

Seam roll and ham: A seam roll is a tightly rolled sausage shape over which you can press sleeves to avoid the seam pressing through from the underside. A ham, as the name suggests, is a tightly stuffed ham shape which is used to press darts, curved areas, folds, etc. so that the fabric retains the shape desired.

GENERAL KIT

Fabric glue: Fray Check is one brand of glue that can be used to dab on thread ends, or where fabric is snipped close to stitching so that it will not fray.

Interfacing and stabilizers: This is a whole subject on its own, but suffice to say, it is a good idea to have a pack of Tearaway stabilizer to hand. This is used to back work that is to be heavily stitched—once stitching is complete, the stabilizer is torn away. Also, a pack or two of fusible interfacing is a good idea. These come in light, medium, and heavy weight to suit different fabrics, and are fused to the back of the material prior to stitching. They provide support and crispness as required for areas such as collars, cuffs, plackets, and pockets.

Ham

PHILIPS

GC 2510

MAX

Steam iron

Interfacing

Optional extras

These may not be essential kit, but the following gadgets, gizmos, and sewing aids certainly make sewing easier and more fun. Because the number of products is so extensive, we have only included the ones we like best.

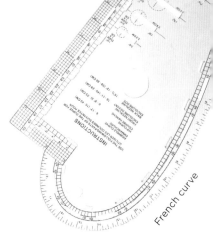

French curve

NIFTY SEWING AIDS

■ **Double-sided fusible webbing:** Usually paper-backed, this is used to fix appliqués to fabric or two fabric pieces back to back. The webbing is fused to the reverse of the appliqué fabric, which is then cut out to shape and the paper backing removed so it can be fused to the right side of the main fabric.

■ **Extension tables:** Many manufacturers make large, flat extension tables that can be fitted snugly to the flatbed of particular sewing machines, which is very useful when sewing large projects like quilts, as the larger, flat surface provides extra support for the mass of fabrics.

■ **Flexible ruler/French curve:** As the name suggests, the flexible ruler bends so you can mark curves easily. A French curve is a transparent flat plastic template with a curved edge with imperial and metric markings.

■ **Finger guard/needle guard:** This is useful if you are teaching children to sew as it helps to prevent fingers getting too close to the needle. Janome's version is a shaped piece of metal that slots into the back of the presser foot ankle and then sits in front of the needle. Husqvarna Viking

has a clear plastic guard that is also attached to the presser foot ankle and sits around the needle like a reverse football goal.

■ **Hemstitch fork:** This looks a little like a tuning fork and is made from metal, with a loop at one end and two long, parallel prongs. It is used to stitch decorative seams that look hand-sewn, such as fagoting. The straight prongs are inserted between two layers of fabric, with the needle falling between the prongs. Increase the stitch length and sew a straight stitch

Horn furniture cabinet

Thimble

Use white paper behind the needle eye
If you don't have a needle threader, hold a piece of white paper behind the needle eye, which makes it easier to see when threading.

Needle threaders

seam, reducing the pressure on the presser foot.

- **Humper jumper—button shank plate/ clearance plate:** A long, fairly thick piece of plastic with an open slot in the center of each end and a bend in the middle, it is used to help sew over bulky seams on coats, denim, etc., to start off more easily at the beginning of a bulky seam, or to create a shank when sewing on buttons.

Humper jumper

- **Needle board/velvet pressing board:** These are used to press pile fabrics and may either be a flexible base with a bed of fine wires into which the pile is pressed so it is not crushed, or a velvet board with a soft pile surface. Again, the nap fabric is pressed with the pile toward the board to prevent the texture being crushed.

- **Needle threaders:** Many modern machines come with an auto needle threader, but there are still occasions when it is necessary to thread needles by eye, including twin needles. This nifty gadget has a tiny hook at one end to make needle threading easier and at the other end a hole to drop the needle in, making it easier to hold while you insert it into the machine.

- **Rouleau loop turner:** A metal or plastic rod with a hook at one end which is used to turn through thin straps easily. The rod is inserted into the strap, which has been stitched right sides together, with the hook latching onto the fabric at the far end so that when the loop is pulled back through the strap, it brings the fabric with it, turning the strap to the right side out.

- **Scissors sharpener:** A very useful gadget to keep scissors pristine and sharp. These devices can be used to quickly sharpen embroidery scissors or dressmaking shears.

SENSIBLE TIMESAVERS

- **Hem marker:** A stand-alone gadget with a chalk puffer that can be moved up and down on a pole, the puffer is attached to a squeezy air ball so you can mark hem allowances easily. The puffer squirts out a thin chalk line at the desired hem height.

- **Thread stand:** Used in addition to the spindles on the sewing machine. The idea is to hold larger or more thread reels, thus saving time when changing threads for multicolor embroideries.

Finger guard

Scissors sharpener

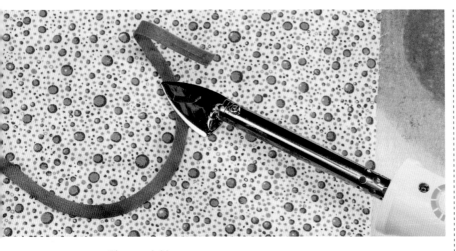

Clover mini iron

■ **Embroidery hoop:** This can be a simple hand-sewing wooden hoop or a specially designed free-motion grip. Use it when free-motion sewing to hold the fabric taut, allowing you to quickly and easily move the fabric in any direction.

■ **Circular attachment:** This is a much simpler version of the circular sewing foot. It is a metal bar with a right angle that slots into the back of the presser foot ankle. Place a drawing pin up through the center of the area that you want to stitch around in a circle and slide the attachment along so that the end is on the pin. Tighten the screw at the back to hold the attachment in place and then stitch a decorative stitch. The fabric will feed in a circle around the pin.

■ **Eyelet plate:** Neat eyelet holes can be stitched perfectly every time when an eyelet plate is used. It fits onto the throat plate and has protruding fingers around which the eyelet is stitched. First, remove the presser foot and ankle, drop the feed dogs, and then make a small hole in the fabric to slot over the finger. Use a small zigzag stitch around the finger, turning the fabric as you stitch. It is easier to stitch if the fabric is in a hoop.

■ **Clover mini iron:** Ideal for pressing small areas such as corners on collars, or seams only on pile fabrics. The clover iron has a little triangular-shaped head to get into small areas.

■ **Rotary cutters and mats:** Essential if cutting long lengths of fabrics for patchworking, etc. The mats are usually self-healing plastic with grids in metric and imperial measurements. Rotary cutters have circular blades to cut through several layers at a time.

CREATIVE SEWING SUPPLIES
■ **Free-motion bobbin holder:** This is simply a spare bobbin holder that looks exactly like the one that is provided in the sewing machine, but is usually preset with lower tension, so is suitable for using with thicker thread on the bobbin. It means you don't have to alter the tension of the existing bobbin holder, which can be tricky to reset for regular sewing. You can also use it for free-motion sewing to produce neater stitching on the underside and for hand-look quilting.

GREAT GIZMOS
■ **Side winder:** A stand-alone bobbin winder that is battery run and thus portable. You can wind almost any bobbin type without having to unthread your sewing machine. Quickly and easily threaded, it will also stop automatically when the bobbin is full.

■ **Bias tape maker:** Bias binding gives a lovely finish to edges, encasing the raw edges of fabric at the same time.

Self-healing cutting board

Rotary cutter

Hand wind heavy thread or textured yarn onto the bobbin

Don't pull the yarn through the bobbin tension. Work with the right side facing down toward the throat plate.

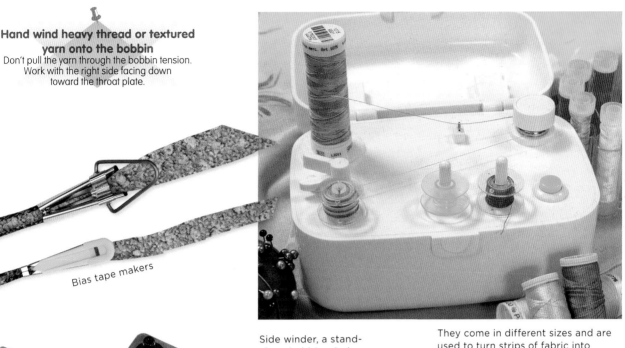

Bias tape makers

Side winder, a stand-alone bobbin winder

Circular attachment

Embroidery hoop

Working with lightweight fabrics

For lightweight fabrics, place work in a hoop and back with a stabilizer.

They come in different sizes and are used to turn strips of fabric into ready-folded bias binding. The fabric strips, cut on the bias, are fed from the wider end and pulled through the narrow end. The gadget folds the long edges of the fabric in toward the middle as it is pulled through. Work on an ironing board and press the folded tape as you pull it from the bias trim maker to hold folds in position.

- **Bias tape making machine:** A useful device if you need to make copious amounts of single-fold bias tape. The full width tape is fed through a tape maker and heated rollers to come out uniformly folded and ready for use. Different width tape makers create different size bindings.

- **Bias tape cutter:** Another device to speed up the process of making bias tape. This one will cut perfectly even lengths of tape to a choice of widths. The fabric is fed through the battery-operated gadget, with a rotary cutter slicing the fabric as it rolls through.

- **Pleater:** A great tool for anyone who enjoys smocking as it reduces the time taken to prepare the pleats. It has a row of evenly spaced needles which need to be threaded before the fabric is fed through a crimped barrel onto the needles. Continue to turn the handle and the fabric will move along through the needles onto the threads into neat and even pleats.

Threads

Many types of thread are available for all kinds of sewing. Strong threads are necessary for making garments and soft furnishings, while decorative threads with more sheen or texture can be used for embellishment.

The raw materials vary. They can be made from natural fibers like cotton or silk, or synthetic/man-made fibers like polyester or rayon. They can even be mixed. The most important factor is to buy good-quality thread for the benefit of your sewing machine and the finished articles.

Change the cones or reels when serging
When serging with four threads, swap the cones or reels occasionally as the loopers use more thread than the needles. Alternating the cones from needles to loopers will even out the usage.

General-purpose sewing thread: May be spun from polyester or mercerized cotton, or have a polyester core covered in cotton. Ideal for making garments, drapes, and other soft-furnishing projects of all fabric types.

Silk thread: Perfect for sewing silk and woolen fabrics as it comes from an animal source. It can be expensive, so polyester thread is a cheaper alternative.

Upholstery thread: Extra strong and made from 100 percent polyester. Ideal for heavy-duty sewing like upholstery and bag making for a secure finish. Fit a size 100/16 needle when sewing with this thread.

Wooly nylon thread: A soft, strong, loosely-spun thread used for serging. Used in the loopers to give better coverage of the seam or edge.

Machine embroidery thread: Fine threads made from rayon or polyester which have a high sheen to reflect the light. Use these reels in conjunction with "bobbin fill" wound on the bobbin.

Bobbin thread: Very fine thread available in black or white and used in the bobbin of machines when doing machine embroidery. Affordable and resourceful—a greater length can be wound onto a bobbin, so that fewer refills are required. Available prewound.

Glow-in-the-dark thread: Used to stitch decorative shapes and embroidered outlines which glow in the dark. A great novelty thread.

Wash-away thread: Used for basting/tacking to hold appliqué and quilting projects while stitching, with the benefit that it will wash away and disappear after it is no longer required.

Select a darker shade of thread
When choosing a thread color to match a fabric, select a slightly darker shade as this will be less noticeable when stitched in place.

Metallic thread: Adds sparkle to your projects. Single and multifilament metallic threads are available on reels. Fit a metallic needle as the larger eye tends not to shred the thread as a standard needle would.

Decorative thread: Come in variegated colors and a range of thicknesses. Fine threads can be used with satin and decorative stitches for an interesting effect and thicker ones can be wound onto the bobbin for reverse sewing or couched on the surface.

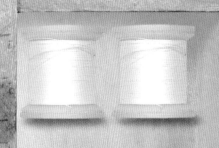

Serger thread: Sergers use a great deal of thread for stitching and neatening seams, so these threads are available on large reels or cones which hold 3,000–17,000ft (1,000–5,000m) of thread. Colors are limited, but a greater choice is available on 3,000ft (1,000m) reels.

Topstitching thread: When stitching is bold and an obvious feature, choose topstitching thread. A strong, heavy thread made from 100 percent polyester. Use for jeans, making buttonholes, and sewing on buttons.

Invisible thread: This fine, flexible filament, which is clear or smoke colored (to match with light and dark fabrics), creates an indiscernible stitch so that the effect is seen without the color.

Smocking thread: Wind onto the bobbin and match with a standard thread in the needle. When the stitching is completed, iron the reverse of the sewing lightly and the bobbin thread shrinks with the heat to form a crinkle effect similar to smocking.

Needles

It is important to use the right type of needle for each project. A wide range of needles is available to suit all tasks, and different types and weights of fabrics and threads. No longer just fine for delicate fabric and thicker for jeans, there is a vast array on sale to improve the stitch finish—the problem is finding the most appropriate one for the job.

ANATOMY OF A NEEDLE

Most needles are a standard fit with a universal shaft to fit almost all machines. However, although needles can all look the same, subtle differences tailor them to specific uses.

Shank: This top part clamps securely into the needle casing of the machine and is held in place with a screw.

Scarf: This is the hollow area at the back of the needle. It allows the bobbin hook to grab the needle thread more easily.

Eye: The hole through which the thread is fed. This varies in size and shape, depending on the type of thread intended for it.

Shaft: The narrow length of the needle which penetrates the fabric.

Point: All points are sharp but some are more rounded than others, and some are chiseled to cut into leather or vinyl.

Groove: The groove in the front of the shaft above the eye allows the thread to sit in it when penetrating the fabric, reducing the drag through the fabric.

Always use a sharp needle
Don't wait until your needle breaks before you change it. A sharp needle will do a much better job than an old blunt one, avoiding skipped stitches and damaged fabric.

NEEDLE SIZE	DESCRIPTION	USE
8/60	Very fine	For fine threads on light and delicate fabrics.
10/70	Fine	For fine threads, and lightweight and sheer fabrics.
12/80	Medium	For medium-weight cottons, synthetics, and mixes.
14/90	General	For heavier fabrics, drapes, and soft-furnishing projects.
16/100	Heavy	For thicker, denser fabrics, drapes, and upholstery projects.
18/110	Extra	For very thick and heavy-weight fabrics sewn with thick threads.

NEEDLES FOR FUNCTIONAL SEWING

TYPE		DESCRIPTION	USE
Standard		Standard needle with a sharp point to penetrate the cloth. Choose the size according to the weight and density of the fabric.	Most weights of woven fabric.
Ballpoint		Rounded point to slide between the fibers rather than split them.	Perfect for knitted fabrics.
Stretch		Deep scarf which prevents skipped stitches.	Stretch fabrics, Lycra/ Spandex, knits, and synthetic suede.
Jeans/denim		Particularly strong and sharp enough to penetrate several layers of denim at once, making it easier to sew over seams—e.g., when shortening the hems of jeans.	Strong, densely woven fabrics like denim or canvas.

NEEDLES FOR DECORATIVE STITCHING

TYPE		DESCRIPTION	USE
Embroidery		A larger eye holds the embroidery thread, and the shape of the scarf allows dense stitching without shredding the thread.	Rayon, polyester, and specialist embroidery threads.
Topstitch		Sharp needle with a large eye and a deep groove in the front of the needle to hold thicker thread when sewing.	Fit this when topstitching.
Metallic		The metallic needle has a large polished eye which holds the thread and prevents it from shredding and skipping stitches.	Use with the range of metallic threads on sale.
Quilting		Sharp point and a tapered shaft.	Designed to sew through multiple thick layers without damaging them.
Twin/Triple		Needles are fixed to one body for fitting into the machine. This allows parallel lines of stitching to be sewn and, as the distance between the needles varies, different effects can be achieved.	Fine pin tucks; to create a shadow effect with colors sewing parallel rows; heirloom/ antique sewing.
Wing		Broad needle with "wings" on either side of the shaft to push the threads apart as the needle enters the fabric to make a hole.	If the needle enters the same place more than once.

Fabric directory

There are far too many different fabrics to include them all here, but we have created six basic categories and taken a few examples of each to give some guidelines on how best to sew them. General advice includes selecting needles and threads, choosing stitch type and size, as well as info on any useful specialist feet.

LIGHTWEIGHT WOVENS

Fabrics described as lightweight may vary in their characteristics, from soft to crisp, or solid to translucent, and each will require specific sewing techniques. In general, however, it is best to use a fine needle and a slightly shorter stitch length. Delicate seams and hems work better than bulky or heavy finishes.

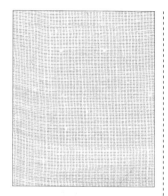

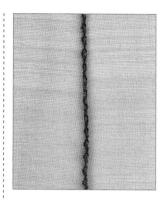

Muslin/calico

- **Description:** Muslin (known as calico in U.K.) is a 100% unbleached cotton fabric available in various weights, from fine lightweight to crisp medium weight. Used to make test garments (toiles), for drapes and craft projects.
- **Thread:** Mercerized cotton.
- **Needle:** Standard 10/70.
- **Stitch:** 10-12spi stitch length (2-2.5mm) for straight stitching, neaten raw edges with zigzag, overcasting, or three-thread serging.
- **Seam:** Plain or French.
- **Useful feet/attachments:** Straight stitch foot; gathering foot for a soft fabric.
- **Notes:** Cut with sharp shears and interface with self-fabric.

Cotton lawn

- **Description:** Smooth, fine, and crisp woven fabric for dresses, shirts, and lingerie. Sometimes used for underlining.
- **Thread:** Mercerized cotton.
- **Needle:** Standard or Microtex, size 10/70 for functional stitching, but consider using a twin or wing needle effect (see page 17).
- **Stitch:** 12spi stitch length (2mm) for straight stitching, neaten with three-thread serging/overlocking, or use a rolled edge.
- **Seam:** Plain or French.
- **Useful feet/attachments:** Straight stitch foot/plate, pin-tuck foot, hemmer foot.
- **Notes:** Cut with long-bladed scissors and use sharp pins; support facings with a lightweight iron-on or sew-in interfacing.

Silk organza

- **Description:** Strong, sheer fabric made from highly spun silk threads.
- **Thread:** Fine thread in silk or polyester.
- **Needle:** Standard or Microtex, size 10/70.
- **Stitch:** 10-12spi stitch length (2-2.5mm) for straight stitching; use a serged/overlocked rolled hem for decorative neatening.
- **Seam:** French or hairline.
- **Useful feet/attachments:** Straight stitch foot/plate.
- **Notes:** Hold layers together with long pins; use a second layer of organza for facings and to give added support without altering the characteristics of the fabric.

Chiffon

- **Description:** Light and soft for blouses, dresses, and scarves. Often used loose in multiple layers.
- **Thread:** Fine silk or polyester thread to match the fiber of the cloth.
- **Needle:** Standard or Microtex, size 10/70.
- **Stitch:** 12spi stitch length (2mm) for straight stitching; use a serged/overlocked rolled edge for decorative hems.
- **Seam:** French or hairline.
- **Useful feet/attachments:** Straight stitch foot/plate, hemmer foot, gathering foot.
- **Notes:** Use long pins and interface with organza to add support.

MEDIUM-WEIGHT WOVENS

For most medium-weight fabrics, use a size 11/80 needle and a standard stitch length of about 10spi stitch length (2.5mm). Choose appropriate presser feet to make sewing tasks easier.

   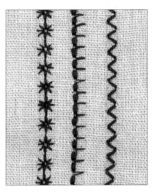

Sheeting

- **Description:** Plain-weave cotton, or polyester/cotton fabric, often available in broader widths for bedding and in many color options.
- **Thread:** Cotton or polyester.
- **Needle:** Standard-point needle, size 10/70 or 12/80.
- **Stitch:** 10spi stitch length (2.5mm) for straight stitching; all types of zigzag, overcasting stitches, and decorative stitches.
- **Seam:** Plain, French, flat fell.
- **Useful feet/attachments:** Zigzag foot for standard sewing; open toe for decorative stitching; walking foot when sewing long seams of printed sheeting to aid pattern matching. Create frills with a ruffle foot.
- **Notes:** Stabilize with a tear-away stabilizer if adding decorative machine stitches; use an iron-on interfacing.

Patchwork cotton

- **Description:** Plain-weave fabric, either plain dyed, batik, or printed for patchwork and quilting projects.
- **Thread:** Cotton for sewing up and quilting thread to finish projects.
- **Needle:** Standard point needle, size 12/80.
- **Stitch:** 10spi stitch length (2.5mm) for straight stitching.
- **Seam:** 1/4in (6mm).
- **Useful feet/attachments:** Quarter-inch foot for accurate seam allowances; walking foot for quilting; stitch-in-the-ditch foot for finishing projects; darning foot for free-hand quilting.
- **Notes:** Use a rotary cutter and mat for accurate cutting.

Silk dupioni

- **Description:** A crisp woven fabric with an uneven surface created by the slubs in the yarn. Although silk has a reputation for being difficult to handle, dupioni is fairly easy to work with.
- **Thread:** Cotton or silk thread (silk is especially good for hand-sewing).
- **Needle:** Standard or Microtex needle, size 10/70 or 12/80.
- **Stitch:** 10spi stitch length (2.5mm) for straight stitching.
- **Seam:** Plain seams to join pieces. Neaten edges with a serger, zigzag stitches, with binding or a Hong Kong finish.
- **Useful feet/attachments:** Zigzag, binding, piping, and overcasting feet are helpful; functional feet and any decorative feet for adding embellishment. Use a ruffle foot for gathering and pleating.
- **Notes:** Cut out all pattern pieces in the same direction. Dupioni frays very easily, so neaten raw edges before sewing up.

Linen

- **Description:** Plain woven linen which wrinkles easily unless treated but has a classic charm. A favorite for shirts, blouses, skirts, pants, and suiting.
- **Thread:** Good-quality cotton thread.
- **Needle:** Standard, size 12/80. Use a topstitch needle for topstitching or a wing needle for a drawn thread effect.
- **Stitch:** 10spi stitch length (2.5mm) for straight stitching and 8spi stitch length (3mm) when topstitching. Machine blanket stitch with a wing needle.
- **Seam:** Plain and flat fell seams.
- **Useful feet/attachments:** Zigzag foot, flat fell foot, an edge stitch foot is helpful when topstitching.
- **Notes:** Neaten edges first as they tend to ravel. Support collar, cuff, and facings with a light iron-on interfacing, which will also help to prevent fraying.

HEAVY-WEIGHT FABRICS

Heavier and thicker fabrics need some special handling to achieve good results. When sewing a thicker cloth, a longer stitch and a stronger needle are required. Use specialist feet to help with particular techniques.

Denim

- **Description:** This traditional blue cloth comes in medium weight but is more often a heavier, stronger material popular for jeans and casual jackets.
- **Thread:** Good-quality cotton for construction and topstitch thread; use a contrasting color to embellish the seams.
- **Needle:** Use a jeans needle (strong enough to penetrate several layers of denim with a large eye for thick thread).
- **Stitch:** 8spi stitch length (3mm) for seaming and topstitching.
- **Seam:** Flat fell and plain seams.
- **Useful feet/attachments:** Flat fell foot when making flat fell seams on jeans; an edge stitch foot when topstitching.
- **Notes:** Use a humper jumper gadget (see page 17) to sew easily over bulky seams.

Tweed

- **Description:** This thick cloth, usually wool, has depth but generally is not very tough. It may be plain or have a check weave.
- **Thread:** General-purpose polyester thread. Hand sew with silk.
- **Needle:** 14/18 (90/110) universal needle.
- **Stitch:** 7-8spi stitch length (3-3.5mm).
- **Seam:** Plain seams pressed flat and neaten the raw edges with a Hong Kong finish or binding.
- **Useful feet/attachments:** A walking foot or roller foot will prevent the thick layers from sliding over each other.
- **Notes:** Wool tweed can stretch and lose its shape—for example, jacket elbows may bag and skirts may seat. Interline (underline) with 100 percent silk organza to help retain the shape.

Home furnishing fabric

- **Description:** Home furnishing or upholstery fabrics include strong, durable materials used for slipcovers, heavy drapes, and cushions.
- **Thread:** Specialist upholstery thread or good-quality polyester.
- **Needle:** 14/18 (90/110) or a jeans needle.
- **Stitch:** 8spi stitch length (3mm). Decorative stitches may be appropriate on smooth-weave plain-colored fabrics.
- **Seam:** Plain seams. Piping or braid is often inserted into the seams to define the shape of, for example, seat pads or headboards.
- **Useful feet/attachments:** A walking foot to feed the layers evenly; large-groove piping foot when piping.
- **Notes:** Use a serger to neaten edges.

Double-faced cloth

- **Description:** Often made of wool fiber, it has two layers joined with central threads. It is very thick as it has two right sides, but this makes it practical for reversible winter coats.
- **Thread:** Silk thread for machining and hand sewing, although polyester is an appropriate alternative.
- **Needle:** Standard size 14/90.
- **Stitch:** 7-8spi stitch length (3-3.5mm).
- **Seam:** Flat fell for reversible garments.
- **Useful feet/attachments:** Walking foot or roller foot to feed the thick layers evenly. Flatlock stitch with decorative thread.
- **Notes:** Use a humper jumper gadget (see page 17) over bulky seams, and sew steadily.

STRETCH

Stretchy fabrics are generally knitted in construction so that as the loops straighten, when they are pulled, the fabric stretches. Specially developed ballpoint/stretch needles, with rounded points, are much more suited to sewing knitted materials, and prevent skipped stitches and fabric damage. Stitch choice is also important as, when straight stitches are stretched with the fabric, the threads often break.

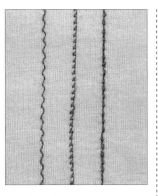

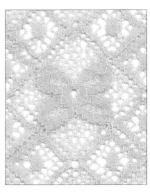

Single knit

- **Description:** Cotton knitted fabric used for T-shirts and underwear. Sometimes Lycra/Elastane is added to improve the stability of the knit.
- **Thread:** Cotton or polyester.
- **Needle:** Ballpoint or stretch needle size 10/12 (70/80).
- **Stitch:** Narrow zigzag or pre-programmed machine stretch stitch.
- **Seam:** Plain sewing machine seam with an overcast stitch to neaten or serged seam. Neaten hems with a rolled or lettuce edge, or topstitch with a twin needle.
- **Useful feet/attachments:** Walking foot or roller foot will feed the fabric evenly without stretching it; an elastic guide foot may be helpful.
- **Notes:** A serger sews stretch fabric well, producing small, neat seams.

Sweat shirting

- **Description:** This thicker stretch cloth sometimes has a softer brushed backing for comfortable leisure clothing.
- **Thread:** Cotton or polyester.
- **Needle:** Ballpoint or stretch needle size 12/14 (80/90), depending on the weight of the cloth.
- **Stitch:** 10spi stitch length (2.5mm) with a serger or sewing machine.
- **Seam:** Use a serger with balanced seams or flatlocking. Alternatively, use plain seams.
- **Useful feet/attachments:** Walking foot or roller foot to feed fabric evenly.
- **Notes:** A serger allows garments to be constructed quickly.

Fleece

- **Description:** Synthetic fleece is a warm, comfortable, and durable fabric without the weight of natural wool. It doesn't fray but it does pill unless treated.
- **Thread:** Polyester.
- **Needle:** Ballpoint or stretch needle size 12/14 (80/90), depending on the weight of the fleece.
- **Stitch:** Use a pre-programmed machine stretch stitch, narrow zigzag, or sew with a serger.
- **Seam:** Plain seams with the raw edges placed to one side and topstitched through all layers, or choose serged seams.
- **Useful feet/attachments:** Walking foot or roller foot for even sewing, or use a serger.
- **Notes:** Mark the wrong side of all fabric pieces with chalk as the sides can look similar.

Stretch lace

- **Description:** Knitted fabric using synthetic and elasticated threads with an intricate pattern built into it.
- **Thread:** Polyester.
- **Needle:** Ballpoint or stretch needle size 12/80.
- **Stitch:** Narrow zigzag or select a sewing machine stretch stitch with wider zigzag for lapped seams.
- **Seam:** Narrow plain seams with the raw edges overcast together, serger seams, or lapped seams.
- **Useful feet/attachments:** Walking foot and roller foot; attach elastic with an elastic guide foot.
- **Notes:** Construction with a serger works well as it is quick, and the seams produced are strong and narrow, so they are less visible through the lace.

SPECIALS
These include fabrics that are particularly difficult to handle and sew due to their construction. Specialist feet are especially useful with this category and have been developed to deal with these features.

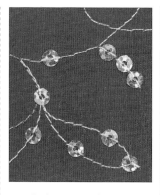

Leather/suede
- **Description:** Prepared, and sometimes dyed, animal skin for garment making.
- **Thread:** Polyester (tannins weaken cotton thread).
- **Needle:** A leather needle has a special point to cut into the tough skin.
- **Stitch:** 7–8spi stitch length (3–3.5mm).
- **Seam:** Plain, welt, or lapped, often topstitched to finish.
- **Useful feet/attachments:** Non-stick, Teflon strips, roller, or walking foot.
- **Notes:** Since this is a natural product, there will be color variations, but cut all pieces in the same direction (using the spine as a grain line) if possible. Use masking tape or weights rather than pins to avoid perforating the skin.

Vinyl
- **Description:** This synthetic product is used on its own or to surface a cotton base fabric and is sometimes textured to imitate leather.
- **Thread:** Polyester.
- **Needle:** Standard or jeans needle size 12/80.
- **Stitch:** 7spi stitch length (3.5mm). Short stitches may weaken the fabric with too many perforations.
- **Seam:** Topstitched welt or lapped seams.
- **Useful feet/attachments:** Non-stick foot or Teflon strips fixed to the underside of a standard foot, roller foot, or walking foot.
- **Notes:** Use masking tape or weights rather than pins to avoid perforating the fabric. If a vinyl garment is to be waterproof, the seams should be taped on the inside to seal them.

Beaded/sequined
- **Description:** A backing fabric of, for example, cotton, velvet, or silk elaborately decorated with embroidery, beads, or sequins. The surface detail makes it necessary to sew the fabric in a different way.
- **Thread:** Match the fiber content of the fabric.
- **Needle:** 10/12 (70/80).
- **Stitch:** 10–12spi stitch length (2–3mm), depending on the weight of the backing cloth.
- **Seam:** Plain seams: remove the beads/sequins from the seam allowance to access the seam line (see Notes below).
- **Useful feet/attachments:** Sew seams with a zip foot so that it sits within the seam allowance and is not impeded by the beads/sequins.
- **Notes:** Save the removed beads/sequins and sew back over the seam if bare areas appear. Use sew-in interfacing to add support to areas that may require it.

Felt
- **Description:** Felted or bonded fabric is neither woven nor knitted, being a mass of fibers matted together; it has no grain or direction.
- **Thread:** Polyester.
- **Needle:** Standard size 12/80.
- **Stitch:** 8–10spi stitch length (2.5–3mm), depending on the thickness of the fabric.
- **Seam:** Felt does not fray. Sew lapped seams and use felt for appliqué.
- **Useful feet/attachments:** Standard straight or zigzag foot for seaming; open toe or appliqué foot for appliqué or decorative sewing.
- **Notes:** Take advantage of the fact that felt does not fray, and just cut and sew it.

PILE

Pile fabrics have additional threads or loops trapped into them which sit on the surface, giving depth and texture to the right side. These fabrics are not suitable for topstitching as the stitches sink into the pile.

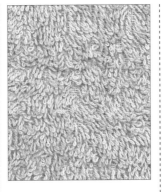

Velvet

- **Description:** This woven fabric can be made from silk, cotton, polyester, or acetate/viscose, and has a dense pile of cut fibers on the surface, giving a luxurious sheen.
- **Thread:** Choose a thread to match the fiber content of the cloth.
- **Needle:** Standard size 10/12 (70/80).
- **Stitch:** 8spi stitch length (3mm).
- **Seam:** Plain seams finger-pressed open.
- **Useful feet/attachments:** A walking foot or roller foot will prevent the layers creeping over each other; invisible zipper foot for inserting zippers.
- **Notes:** Sew with the pile, not against it, and insert an invisible zipper rather than one requiring topstitching. Press carefully, using a needle board (page 17), to avoid flattening the pile. Use sew-in interfacing.

Corduroy

- **Description:** This fabric has characteristic stripes or bands of pile on the surface which may form delicate needlecord fabric or broader "elephant" or "whale" cord.
- **Thread:** Cotton.
- **Needle:** Standard fine needle, size 12/80, for needlecord, and a stronger jeans needle for heavier weights.
- **Stitch:** 10spi stitch length (2.5mm) for needlecord and 8spi stitch length (3mm) for broader cords.
- **Seam:** Plain seams neatened with an overcast stitch, zigzag, or serger; flat fell seams.
- **Useful feet/attachments:** Zigzag foot, overcast foot, walking foot, roller foot, and flat fell foot.
- **Notes:** Cut all pieces in the same direction and sew with, not against, the pile.

Terrycloth

- **Description:** 100 percent cotton fabric with loops of thread on both sides to increase the surface area and improve the absorbency of the cloth. Generally used to make towels and robes.
- **Thread:** Cotton.
- **Needle:** Standard needle size 12/14 (80/90), depending on thickness.
- **Stitch:** 8spi stitch length (3mm).
- **Seam:** Plain seams with raw edges neatened together or serged seams.
- **Useful feet/attachments:** Zigzag foot, overcast foot, walking foot, roller foot.
- **Notes:** Not suitable for decorative stitching, since the stitches will be lost in the pile. After cutting out, vacuum the tiny loose fibers.

Faux fur

- **Description:** Synthetic fur fabric can be created to imitate various types of animal fur with shorter or longer pile. Use it for coats, jackets, bags, and costumes.
- **Thread:** Polyester thread.
- **Needle:** Standard needle size 12/80 for shorter pile; 14/90 for longer pile.
- **Stitch:** Stitch with a zigzag approximately 8spi stitch length (3mm) wide by 8spi stitch length (3mm) long.
- **Seam:** Cut away the seam allowance, then zigzag over the cut edges for a flat seam finish.
- **Useful feet/attachments:** Zigzag foot, walking foot, roller foot.
- **Notes:** Cut with short-bladed scissors, snipping only the backing fabric, then pull the pile apart. Keep the vacuum cleaner to hand to control any loose fibers.

CHAPTER 2
Basic feet

All sewing machines come with a selection of presser feet—how many depends on the brand, model, and cost of the sewing machine. What is certain is that even a beginner's sewing machine will have a choice of straight/zigzag foot, zipper foot, and buttonhole foot. Many will also have overcast and blind hem feet. These, together with hemmer and button sewing feet, can all be classed as "basic." In this chapter, we showcase this essential collection, armed with which you can sew and neaten seams, add decorative topstitching, insert zippers, add piping, beading, and trims, create invisible hems or the tiniest hem on transparent fabrics, and very quickly sew on button after button with ease.

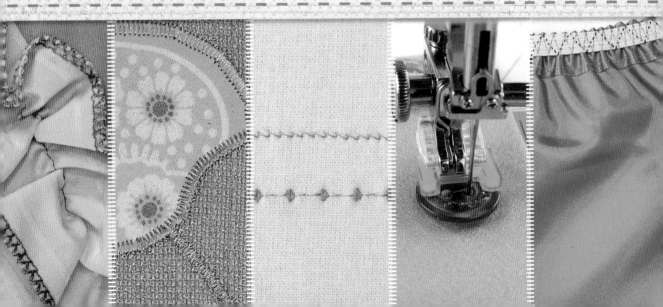

Straight stitch foot

Classic Janome straight stitch foot

A straight stitch foot is used to sew simple straight stitch seams, in particular on very fine or very heavy fabrics. Not only can it be used to sew regular seams, it is also ideal for topstitching, sewing darts, etc. The small hole through which the needle passes gives support around the needle to prevent skipped stitches and puckering.

WHAT A STRAIGHT STITCH FOOT LOOKS LIKE

The foot will have two toes and a flat underside which provide an even pressure against the feed dogs, helping to guide fabrics smoothly. It will also have a fairly small central needle hole.

HOW A STRAIGHT STITCH FOOT WORKS

Quite simply, the straight stitch foot helps to feed the fabrics through the feed dogs smoothly as you sew a straight seam. It is particularly useful for very lightweight fabrics such as chiffon, silks, georgette, etc., which otherwise might bunch up or get pulled down into the feed dogs.

   If your machine comes with both zigzag stitch and straight stitch feet, it is likely that the zigzag foot will be attached to the machine when it arrives in the box (see page 34). If it is a combined straight/zigzag foot, it will be in place as it is the most regularly used foot.

Draw a chalk line
Draw a chalk line to follow when topstitching or sewing darts.

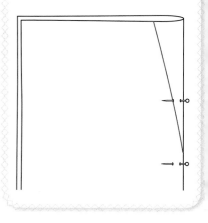

Make sideways stitches too
On some basic sewing machines, the straight stitch and zigzag foot are one and the same, so the central hole will be larger to enable sideways stitches.

SEWING WITH A STRAIGHT STITCH FOOT

Use this foot if you are sewing lightweight fabrics such as chiffon, silk, georgette, or heavyweight, smoothly woven fabrics such as denim, flannel, or worsted wool.

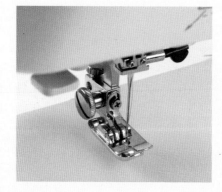

1 Attach the foot to the holder and check that the needle is in the center position (this can be done by changing the stitch selection). Lower the needle down through the foot by turning the balance wheel on the side of the sewing machine by hand.

2 Select a straight stitch from your choice of stitches. Again, check that the needle will go down through the hole in the foot by turning the balance wheel by hand.

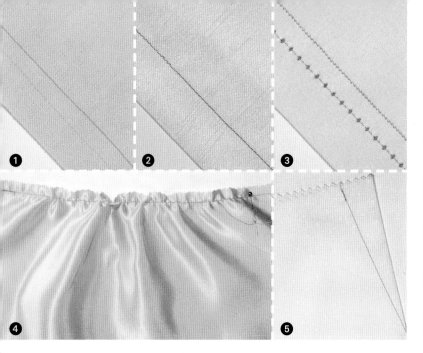

① ② ③

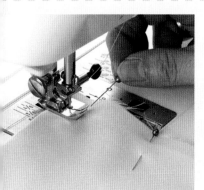

④ ⑤

Straight stitch needle plate

Also known as a straight stitch throat plate, this can be used in conjunction with a straight stitch foot. It has a small round hole for the needle to go through, making it much easier to sew lightweight fabrics without the risk of them being pulled down into the feed dogs or for free-motion machine embroidery with straight stitch. Remove the regular throat plate by unscrewing the retaining screws and insert the straight stitch plate. The plate is not available for all types of sewing machine.

IDEAS FILE

1 Topstitching: A straight stitch foot can be used to topstitch, either in a matching color as a practical aid to hold facings and hems in place, or in a contrast color to stand out and add detail.

2 Two threads for topstitching: Make topstitching really stand out by using two top threads. If you have two thread spindles, put one on each and then through the thread path together. If you have only one thread spindle, put a bobbin of thread on top of the single thread spindle.

3 Use a different straight stitch selection for decorative topstitching: Try out different straight stitch patterns available on some machines to make topstitching really stand out. This is great for attaching patch pockets or adding detail to collars and cuffs. (Note: a stretch stitch or very small zigzag stitch pattern may be possible—check the needle doesn't hit the side of foot or throat plate by turning the balance wheel to lower and raise the needle through the stitch sequence.)

4 Gather stitch on lightweight fabrics: Set the stitch length to the longest possible (or select the gather stitch) and sew in the seam allowance, just outside seam line. Back stitch at the start of the gathering to secure the thread and leave a long thread tail at the other end. Use the bobbin thread to pull up the gathers. If gathering fabric lengths longer than 20in (51cm), stitch the row in two parts and gather each separately.

5 Sew darts on lightweight fabric: Use the straight stitch foot to sew darts neatly. Start at the garment edge and widest part of the dart and taper to the fold at the tip.

5 Sew straight seam, adjusting the stitch length if needed to suit the fabric—for lightweight fabrics, 2.2–2.5; for heavyweight fabrics, 3–3.5. Press the seam before stitching over it again. Neaten any raw edges (see zigzag foot).

4 At the start and end of the seam, back stitch/ reverse stitch or fix/lock stitch by stitching on the spot to secure the seam.

3 With fabric layers right sides together, place the fabric under the foot so that the raw edges are aligned with the ⁵⁄₈in (15mm) guide line on the throat plate.

Classic Janome
zigzag foot

Zigzag foot

This is the most commonly used foot for general sewing techniques. It can be used for all sorts of stitching, from straight seaming to decorative stitches on all weights of fabric. It is particularly designed for sideways stitches, which include simple zigzag and satin stitch to more complex decorative patterns.

The zigzag foot
This is usually the foot that is already attached to the sewing machine when purchased.

WHAT A ZIGZAG FOOT LOOKS LIKE

This foot can be in metal or clear plastic and will have two toes evenly spaced so the foot holds the material down evenly to produce an even stitch pattern. There is a large, centered, oval-shaped hole so the needle can be used in any position. On the underside is a small indentation so that it can glide easily over concentrated stitching.

HOW A ZIGZAG FOOT WORKS

The large oval-shaped hole through which the needle goes means that the needle can swing from side to side easily without hitting the side of the presser foot as you stitch out decorative patterns. It also means that you can decide the needle position, and stitch with the needle to the far right, far left, or anywhere in between (depending on how many needle positions your machine has).

For instance, this makes edge stitching close to the edge of the fabric easier, as the foot will still hold the fabric evenly, but the needle can be to the far right, thus stitching closer to the edge. The indentation on the underside means that, when producing concentrated stitches such as satin stitch (zigzag stitch with the width set to very close, 0.3 or 0.5), the foot will glide over the raised stitching very easily.

The Universal zigzag foot is available to fit most brands.

The "catch-all" foot
The zigzag stitch foot is the "catch-all" foot and can be used for all general sewing applications

SEWING WITH A ZIGZAG FOOT

Use this foot for most general sewing applications, on all fabric weights, particularly when sewing with a zigzag or other sideways stitch.

1 Attach the foot and then select a zigzag stitch. When sewing on stretch fabrics, use a stretch or small zigzag stitch to sew the seams. This will ensure that there is still some stretch in the seams, necessary for pulling a garment on and off.

2 Adjust the stitch width to change the sideways length of the stitch and stitch the length to spread stitches out for lightweight fabrics. Use a larger stitch width and length for medium to heavy fabrics.

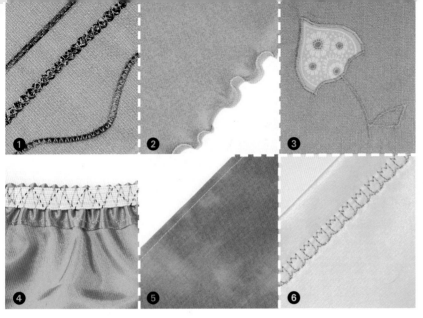

Versatility of the zigzag foot

The zigzag foot is the most versatile foot available as it can be used for all general sewing. The clear-view versions are preferable, as you can see the stitches being formed more easily. When using this foot with twin needles or two-stitch wide decorative stitch patterns, check that the needles will not hit the side of the presser foot or throat plate by turning the balance wheel by hand for the whole of the stitch sequence. If it does rub against the side, reduce the stitch width slightly to reduce the sideways length of the stitches.

IDEAS FILE

1 Couch down yarns: Lay yarns or ribbons on the surface of a cloth and zigzag stitch over them with a zigzag or triple zigzag stitch to couch down the threads.

2 Lettuce edging: On stretch fabrics, zigzag stitch with a small length and width stitch, with the right swing of the stitch falling off the fabric edge and gently stretching the fabric behind and in front of the needle as you sew.

3 Satin stitch edges: Decrease the stitch length to a very narrow 0.3 or 0.5 so that the stitches are formed very close together to cover the edges of appliqués, create letters, or to stitch fabric edges.

4 Attach elastic easily: Use a triple zigzag stitch to attach elastic. Cut the elastic to the length required, then stretch it as you stitch in place with the stitch length increased so that when the elastic falls back to its natural position, the stitching doesn't pucker.

5 Move needle position and edge stitch: This allows you to stitch closer to the edge of the fabric while the fabric is still held under the foot.

6 Stitch decorative patterns: Use this foot for decorative sideways stitch patterns and those with concentrated stitching so that the foot helps to feed the fabric evenly as you sew.

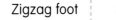

3 Adjust the stitch length to change how close the stitches are formed together. The closer they are, the more fabric is covered completely, useful for covering fabric edges. Stitch so that the right swing of the needle is just off the edge of the fabric.

4 Use a zigzag stitch to neaten raw edges of seam allowances, then trim the fabric close to the stitching.

5 Use this foot with a twin needle to stitch two parallel rows of straight or zigzag stitching in one pass. When selecting a stitch, turn the balance wheel by hand to ensure that the needle doesn't hit the side of the presser foot.

The foot can be moved either side of the needle

Invisible zipper feet may be chunky and rectangular (top: Janome) or slimmer and tapered toward the front (bottom: Brother).

Zipper foot

Primarily of course, zipper feet are used to insert zippers. However, they are also useful for attaching piping and beaded or fringed trims where it is necessary to stitch close to the bulky beading, without the foot getting in the way.

WHAT A ZIPPER FOOT LOOKS LIKE
Basic zipper feet can look very different from each other, but they do the same job. Most common is the single prong with an indent either side. Others may have a wider base, but again with indents either side. The foot is attached either side of the shank, depending on which side of the zipper is being sewn. Janome have an adjustable zipper foot which can be moved along a bar to get as close to the zipper teeth or trim as possible. The zipper foot is useful for attaching any trim with a bulky decorative edging as you can get closer to the edge because of the indents in the foot that allow the needle to be closer.

Regular zipper and zipper foot

Concealed zipper and underside of the invisible-zipper foot

Opening the zipper
After the zipper is basted in place, remove the seam-basting stitches, allowing you to open the zip for the final stages.

SEWING A REGULAR ZIPPER
Position the zipper on a basted seam, edges pressed flat to either side, and follow these steps.

2 Working on the wrong side of fabric, place the zipper face down over the seam allowances, with teeth centered over the basted seam. Pin and baste in place through all layers down both sides of the zipper tape. Remove pins.

3 Turn fabric to right side. Attach the zipper foot, so that the needle is close to the zipper teeth—position to left or right to ensure needle goes down through indent of the foot, avoiding the zipper teeth. Turn the balance wheel by hand for the first few stitches to ensure the needle will not hit the foot.

1 Mark the position of the zipper in the seam allowance, marking from the top of the teeth to the base of the zipper teeth. Baste the seam to bottom mark, changing to regular stitch length to sew the rest of the seam. Press seam open.

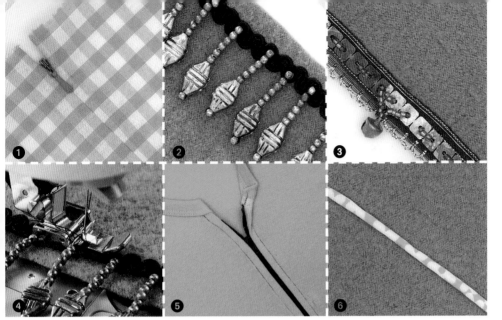

IDEAS FILE
1 Hidden fastenings: Get a 100% concealed invisible zipper.
2,3 & 4 Edge trims: Beaded fringe and sequined trim, surface mounted (see over the page). The zipper foot allows trims to be applied at the edge.
5 Neat details: Visible zippers can add design detailing—note the contrast color thread.
6 Piping: Can be attached neatly in the seam.

ATTACHING BEADED FRINGING

The zipper foot is useful for attaching any trim with a bulky decorative edging as you can get closer to the edge as the indents allow the needle to be positioned closer to the raised edge. A trim with a pretty tape can be surface mounted so that all of the trimming is visible.

INVISIBLE ZIPPER FOOT

Concealed zippers have the teeth on the underside of the zipper. They are sewn to the seam allowances only, so there is no visible stitching on the front of the garment. This is possible with the use of an invisible zipper foot. This has a small hole underneath for the needle to go through, and two deep channels in which the zipper teeth sit so that you stitch extremely closely to them. An invisible zipper foot is essential to insert a truly "invisible" zipper (see next page for more).

4 Starting at the seam at the bottom of the zipper, stitch approximately $^3/_8$in (1cm) from seam, at right angles to zipper. With needle down, raise presser foot and pivot work to stitch up side of zipper tape. As you near the top and the zipper pull, stop with needle down, raise the presser foot and gently work the zipper pull down beyond the needle and presser foot. Continue to sew to end of tape. Fix stitches, then cut thread.

5 Move presser foot to other side of shank so other indent will be closest to teeth and then starting from the bottom of the zipper at seam line again, repeat for other side of zipper. Remove remaining basting stitches.

WHAT AN INVISIBLE ZIPPER FOOT LOOKS LIKE

This foot will have two deep grooves on the underside through which the teeth of the invisible zipper are fed. In the center is a small hole for the needle. Brands may vary (see page 36).

HOW AN INVISIBLE ZIPPER FOOT WORKS

Unlike the regular zipper foot, which sits next to the raised zipper teeth, this special foot with deep grooves sits over the zipper, with the teeth running through one of the grooves. You must use the center needle position, so that the stitching will form very close to the zipper teeth. If possible, depending on the make of sewing machine, you can move the needle position slightly to get almost under the teeth which will be pushed slightly away from the needle as you stitch. A Universal roller concealed zipper foot is available to fit most brands.

SEWING AN INVISIBLE ZIPPER

Concealed zippers are perfect for skirts and dresses. Inserted into the seam at center back or side, they provide an invisible closure as no stitching is shown on the right side of the garment.

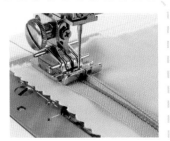

1 Press the seam allowances to the wrong side to form creases at the seam line. Unfold. Unlike a conventional zipper, the seam is not stitched until after the zipper is inserted.

2 With left garment section right side up, open the zipper and place the left zipper tape on the seam allowance, with the zipper teeth along the seam line. Using a regular zipper foot, baste in place down the center of the zipper tape. Note: You cannot stitch the last 1in (2.5cm) because the zipper has to be open when stitched and thus the zipper pull is in the way.

3 Change the foot to an invisible zipper foot and, starting from the top of the zipper, position over the zipper so the teeth fit into one of the grooves underneath. Take one or two stitches by turning the balance wheel by hand. Once you are satisfied that the needle goes through the hole clearly and is stitching very close to the teeth, stitch down to as close as possible to the bottom.

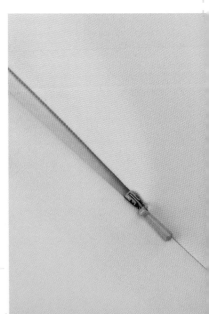

4 Attach the right zipper tape to the right side of the right seam allowance in the same manner.

5 Attach a regular zipper foot and, with fabric right sides together, stitch the remainder of the seam, starting where the zipper stitching finished. Don't forget, you can move the needle position so that the stitching lines up more easily.

Buttonhole foot

Buttonholes are far easier to stitch successfully nowadays because many sewing machines have simple stepped buttonhole stitch selections combined with a purpose-made buttonhole foot. Some models will have a foot into which the button is also placed, and then the hole is stitched to fit that button, making it even simpler to stitch the right size hole every time.

Janome buttonhole foot with extension

Husqvarna Viking model

Test your buttonholes first
Always interface the buttonhole area and test the buttonholes on a fabric scrap first, with the same number of layers you intend to use with it, to check how it looks and which way it sews the first side—toward you or away from you.

WHAT A BUTTONHOLE FOOT LOOKS LIKE

There are two main types of buttonhole foot. One is generally made from white plastic and has a long sliding extension to the back into which a button can be placed. The foot is then snapped or clipped to the foot holder in the usual way, and the buttonhole stitched to fit the button in the foot. The other buttonhole foot has two evenly spaced toes, with indentations on the underside so the foot glides easily over the dense satin stitch that makes up the buttonhole stitching.

HOW A BUTTONHOLE FOOT WORKS

Buttonholes are stitched in four to six steps: bar tack one end, satin stitch down one side, bar tack at the other end, satin stitch back to the beginning, and fix stitch to finish. Some models will add a further two steps, stitching a straight line after bar tacking and before satin stitching the sides. On some machines the whole buttonhole can be stitched in one step, while with other machines you need to adjust the stitch selection for each of the four steps. On basic or non-computerized models, you may also have to decide on the buttonhole length, stopping when you have reached the length marked on the fabric before selecting the next step in the sequence. On computerized models with a simple buttonhole foot, you can select the length on the LCD screen to stitch out automatically. On the button-holding foot, the amount the extension is open to fit the button is the length that the buttonhole will automatically stitch.

SEWING BUTTONHOLES

Perfectly stitched buttonholes are a breeze when sewn with a purpose-made buttonhole foot. If like the one shown here, the size of the hole is automatically made to fit the button slotted in the back.

1 Mark the buttonhole position on the fabric. Slide the extension on the button-holding foot open as far as it will go and insert the button in the back of the foot, closing the extension to hold the button securely. If using a regular buttonhole foot on a computerized machine, measure the diameter of the button, add 1/8in (3mm), and select this as the buttonhole length. For basic machines, chalk mark the desired length on the fabric.

2 Put the foot on the machine (if applicable, so that the button is at the back). Pull down the lever to the left so it butts up against the foot (see sewing machine User's Manual) and select the buttonhole stitch you prefer. There is often a choice of up to seven different styles.

CONTINUED NEXT PAGE

Buttonhole know-how

Mark a vertical buttonhole with chalk, making a line from the top to the bottom of the buttonhole position, and then mark each buttonhole length evenly spaced along the line. Mark the top of each buttonhole in one color and the bottom in a different color so it is easy to see the difference between the buttonholes and the spaces between them. For horizontal buttonholes, draw two parallel lines in the buttonhole position so that the distance between them is the buttonhole length. Mark buttonholes evenly spaced, like rungs of a ladder.

Sew-through buttons   Shank buttons

Sew-through and shank buttons

A sew-through button has two or four holes through which you sew to attach it to the fabric below. A shank button has a loop on the underside through which you sew to attach the button in place. No thread shows on the right side of the shank button.

To cut open a buttonhole

Insert a pin at one end, close to the bar tack, and, working from the other end, push the sharp point of a quick unpick between the rows of stitching, pushing it carefully toward the pin at the other end.

To determine the buttonhole length

When measuring buttons to determine the buttonhole length required, add ⅛in (3mm) for ease.

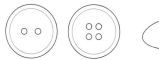

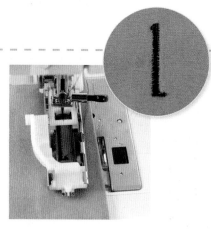

3 If making a four-step buttonhole, select the first step on the stitch selector to stitch the first step (this may be the bar tack at one end, or the first side) and adjust the stitch length to about 0.3–0.5 (the optimum position is usually marked on the sewing machine). For one-step buttonholes, just select the buttonhole from the stitch selector.

4 For a four-step buttonhole, select the next step of the buttonhole and stitch the next phase. If necessary, adjust the stitch length to make the stitches closer together. Stitch to the length required or, if using a button-holding foot, stitch until it stops.

5 Continue to change the stitch selector to stitch the end bar tack and the second side, then fix the stitch, taking the thread tails through to the back, knot, and feed the ends through the stitching along one side. To make the next buttonhole, move the fabric to the next marked position, then change the stitch selection to straight stitch, then back to the first step of the buttonhole to reset the sewing machine to start again.

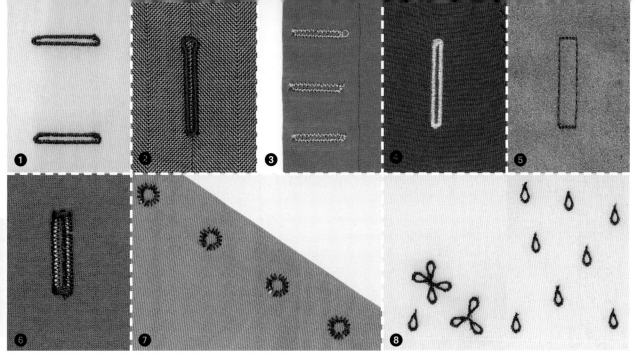

IDEAS FILE

1 Buttonholes on transparent fabric: On lightweight transparent fabric, interface the buttonhole area with beige/nude interfacing or another layer of fashion fabric, adding a soluble layer of stabilizer underneath, which is washed away once the buttonhole is stitched.

2 Keyhole buttonholes: For coats and jackets, stitch a keyhole buttonhole to combine button with a shank (loop on the reverse that stands away from the fabric), providing enough room for the second layer of fabric to lie flat once buttoned up.

3 Hand-stitched look: If making buttonholes on fabrics that don't fray, select a more open-stitched buttonhole.

4 Design feature: Stitch buttonholes out in a contrast color cotton.

5 For leather and suede: A straight stitch buttonhole is preferable. The material doesn't fray and it uses the minimum of stitching, thus making the minimum of holes in the dense fabric.

6 Corded buttonhole: For a more substantial and raised buttonhole, or when making buttonholes on stretch fabric, stitch over cording (see below).

7 Eyelets: Use a zigzag foot and stitch eyelet buttonholes for lacing. Cut open with an awl.

8 Create a pattern: Use a tear drop buttonhole as a design feature. Same colored thread creates a subtle design; contrast thread will make it stand out.

CORDED BUTTONHOLES

A corded buttonhole is simply one that is stitched over a fine cord, making it more robust and slightly raised for greater definition. These are useful for knit fabrics that might stretch or bulky heavyweight fabrics.

1 Loop a length of cord, heavy thread, or perle cotton around the hook at the back of the buttonhole foot, holding the ends taut at the front (some buttonhole feet also have guides at the front to hold the cords taut).

2 Holding the threads evenly at the front, stitch the first half of the buttonhole so that the satin stitching for the sides sews over the cord, concealing it beneath the stitching.

3 Stitch the remainder of the buttonhole and, when finished, carefully unloop cord at the end and remove from the machine. Gently pull on one of the cord ends until the loop at the other end disappears into the stitching.

4 Either feed the cord through to the reverse of the fabric and under the stitching, or cut the ends very close to bar tack.

Janome button sewing foot

Button sewing foot

The button foot simply holds the button in position while you sew a zigzag stitch between the holes.

WHAT A BUTTON SEWING FOOT LOOKS LIKE
This is a small, rectangular-shaped foot with a large stitching hole in the center of two thick toes. Usually made from either clear plastic or blue plastic, it may also come with a separate clearance plate which helps you add a thread shank to the stitching so that the button is loose enough for the fabric to lie flat when buttoned up. The clearance plate will have a thick and thin end.

HOW A BUTTON SEWING FOOT WORKS
In order to stitch on the spot, without feeding the fabric and button as you stitch, it is necessary to lower the feed dogs (see your User's Manual to find out how this is done on your machine). If it comes with a clearance plate, insert the thin end below the button for lightweight fabrics and the thick end under for heavyweight fabrics. This will cause the stitching to be loose so that the excess can be wrapped with thread under the button to form a button shank.

Universal button sewing foot available to fit most brands.

Sewing a four-hole button
Once the first two holes are stitched, raise the presser foot and turn the button so that the remaining two holes are in the horizontal position. Stitch through them in the same manner, taking six to eight stitches.

SEWING ON BUTTONS
A button sewing foot makes quick work of attaching a row of sew-through buttons securely and neatly. Usually provided as a standard foot, it holds the button in place as you zigzag stitch through the holes.

1 Attach the button sewing foot and lower the feed dogs so that they will not try to feed the fabric as you sew. Position the button under the foot with two holes aligned horizontally.

2 Select zigzag stitch and then turn the balance wheel by hand, adjusting the button position to ensure the needle goes through the first hole.

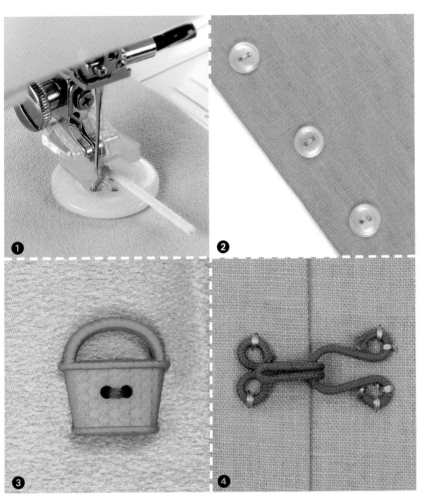

IDEAS FILE

1 Make a thread shank: Use the clearance plate provided, slipping it under the button before stitching. Alternatively, hold a toothpick or matchstick in the center of the button as you stitch over it between the holes. Leave a long thread tail and, once stitched, take the thread to the back of the button close to stitching and wrap the tail around the loose thread shank. Take the rest of the thread to the reverse of the work and tie off.

2 Stitch on a row of buttons: You can do this really quickly using the button sewing foot.

3 Use a contrast color thread: And attach a button to make a design feature out of the fastening.

4 Attach a large hook-and-eye fasteners

Holding the button in position

Many machines come with a button sewing foot which holds the button in position when lowered. It only works with flat sew-through buttons (not those with a shank). It is very useful if you have a number of flat sew-through buttons to attach.

3 Continuing to turn the balance wheel by hand, lower the needle toward the second hole. If it hits the side of the button, adjust the stitch width until it misses the sides and slides clearly through the hole.

4 Zigzag stitch button in place with six to eight stitches. Fix the stitch or take the thread ends to reverse and tie off.

Janome blind
hem foot

Underside of
Janome blind
hem foot

Janome
adjustable
blind hem foot

Blind hem foot

A blind hem foot is specifically designed to make stitching blind hems easy and virtually invisible when combined with a blind hem stitch, which is a basic utility stitch found on all modern sewing machines.

WHAT A BLIND HEM FOOT LOOKS LIKE

Most blind hem feet will have a metal guide in the center and slight indentations on the underside. The guide protrudes below the two toes of the foot to form a little ledge. Some blind hem feet don't have this contrast metal guide but have a narrow toe and a wider toe, the inner edge of which rides along the folded hem edge.

HOW A BLIND HEM FOOT WORKS

The hem allowance is folded up and back on itself so a scant 1/4–1/2in (6–13mm) sits to the right and the fold is butted against the protruding metal guide or edge of the foot's right-hand toe. The blind stitch, which is a row of straight stitches followed by a regular zigzag stitch, is formed mainly in the hem allowance, with the left swing of the zigzag stitch just catching in the

fold of the fabric. The guide keeps the fold and stitching in a straight line. From the right side, all that is visible is a small line of vertical stitches.

A universal blind hem foot is available to fit most brands.

For a near-invisible finish
Select a thread color that matches the fabric as closely as possible to ensure a near-invisible finish.

SEWING WITH A BLIND HEM FOOT

A blind hem is a perfect technique for medium- to heavyweight fabrics, providing a neat, almost invisible finish.

1 Neaten the raw edge of the hem allowance and then fold up at the hem line. Keep the fold in place, refold the hem allowance back under the garment so that just 1/2in (13mm) of the hem edge is to the right.

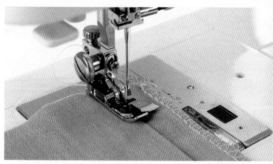

2 Attach the blind hem foot and position the pinned fabric under the foot so the garment is to the left, with the fold butted up against the metal guide on the foot.

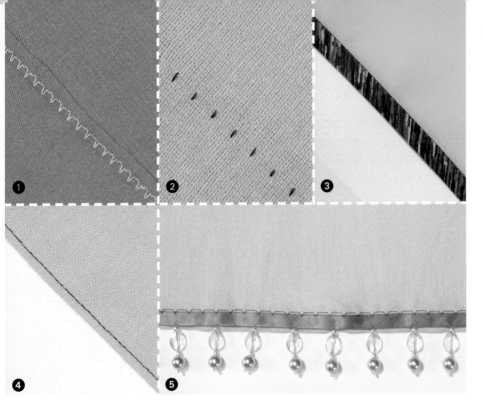

① ② ③ ④ ⑤

Blind hemming tips

The key to an invisible blind hem stitch is to use a thread that perfectly matches the fabric and to ensure that the left swing of the zigzag stitch only just catches in the fold of the fabric, thus making the tiniest of ladder stitches. If a perfect thread color isn't available, choose a slightly darker shade as it will appear lighter when unraveled as a single strand. On open weave or loosely woven fabrics, add weight and stability to the hem allowance by fusing some interfacing in place before turning up the hem.

IDEAS FILE

1 Hemming stretch fabric: On stretch fabrics, use the stretch blind hem stitch, which has a small zigzag stitch in the hem allowance, and wider zigzag stitch to catch the fold of the fabric.

2 Make the stitch a feature: Choose a contrast color thread so that the little ladder stitch on the right side is purposefully visible.

3 Stitch in the ditch: (or stitch in the seam of a previously stitched row.) Use the metal guide on the blind hem foot as a guide to stitch in the ditch, invisibly attaching the underside of the bias binding to neaten the neckline or armholes.

4 Edge stitch: Use the blind hem foot to edge stitch, with the guide running down the edge of the foot and the stitching forming to the left, close to the fabric edge (move the needle to the far left).

5 Add trim to the hem: Fold up a narrow double hem and then, from the right side, blind stitch a beaded trim in place, stitching the hem at the same time (increasing the stitch width to the widest possible to catch the trim).

3 Select the blind hem stitch. Turn the balance wheel by hand to test and ensure that the straight stitch part of the blind hem stitch will fall on the hem allowance only. The zigzag stitch should fall just inside the fold of fabric. If it falls too far to the left, decrease the stitch width slightly. If the zigzag stitch is not catching the fold, increase the stitch width slightly. Continue to the end of the hem.

4 Fold the hem allowance back to the correct position and then press to embed the stitches, avoiding pressing the very edge of the hem, which should be left slightly rounded.

Hemmer foot

Rolled or narrow hems are found in almost all areas of sewing, from soft furnishings to dressmaking, and provide a very professional-looking result. Also known as a rolled hem foot or picot hem foot, a hemmer foot is designed to help stitch a narrow double hem in one pass. Different size hemmer feet are available to suit different fabric weights.

The perfect finish
Narrow/rolled hems are the perfect finish for table linen, shirt tails, chiffon overskirts, and dresses.

The coils in the front of a hemmer foot come in different sizes to make wider or narrower hems where desired.

WHAT A HEMMER FOOT LOOKS LIKE
This foot has an angled, curled scroll at the front through which the fabric is fed so that it curls the raw edge under as it feeds through. On the underside is an indentation to help smoothly feed the folded layers of fabric. For lightweight fabrics, the hemmer has a $1/32$–$1/16$in (1–2mm) scroll and indentation; for medium- and heavyweight fabrics, it has a larger scroll of $1/8$–$1/4$in (4–6mm). Many hemmer feet come in packs of two to cater for different fabric weights.

HOW A HEMMER FOOT WORKS
A narrow hem is formed by turning under a scant $1/16$–$1/4$in (2–6mm) of fabric twice so that the raw edge is completely encased. With this foot, the raw fabric edge is fed into the scroll at the front of the hemmer where it curls, tucking the raw edge under as it continues to curl to form the double hem turn, which is then stitched in place as it passes beneath the foot. Because there is an indentation on the underside, the foot glides smoothly over the increased layers of the hem allowance. The width of the scroll on the front of the foot and the indentation underneath will determine how narrow the hem is. The indentation is the width of the finished narrow hem. The Universal rolled hem foot is available to fit most brands.

SEWING WITH A HEMMER FOOT
A rolled hem, stitched with a hemmer foot, provides a very neat finish, with the minimum of bulk as it is formed from very little fabric. It is perfect for lightweight and transparent fabrics.

1 Because a rolled hem takes very little hem allowance first cut off any excess hem allowance, leaving just $1/4$–$1/2$in (6–13mm). Press up half this hem allowance, then fold the same amount again along the first 6in (15cm). Pin in place at the start.

2 Place the fabric under the foot, wrong side uppermost, stitch for about $1/2$in (13mm) and then gently pull the folded edge of the hem allowance into the scroll of the foot.

3 Stitch slowly, checking that the fabric is curling completely in the scroll, and the raw edge is getting tucked neatly inside before being stitched.

IDEAS FILE

1 Use a zigzag stitch: To stitch the rolled hem in place. This is particularly suitable for fine narrow hems on lightweight fabrics or stretch fabrics, and causes the hem to roll nicely rather than lie flat.

2 To create a scalloped rolled hem edge: Stitch with an heirloom stitch such as a shell stitch.

3 Sew with decorative stitches: When using the wider ⅛–¼in (4–6mm) hemmer foot, you can use decorative stitches to finish the hem.

4 Couch yarns: Use the scroll in the rolled hem foot to feed through yarns and threads that can be couched down on the fabric surface. Anchor in place with a triple zigzag stitch.

5 Create surface texture: Add surface detail with a cord fed through a wider hemmer ⅛–¼in (4–6mm) and cover the cord with satin stitch (stitch length approximately 0.35 and width to cover the cord side to side).

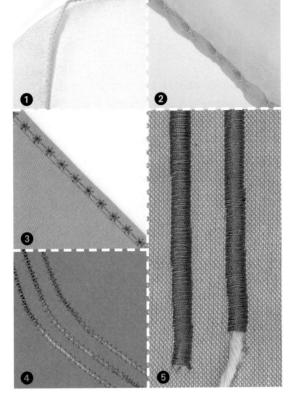

Make it easy to feed the fabric through the scroll

If you find it difficult to feed the fabric evenly through the scroll at the start, stitch the first 1in (2.5cm) without going through the scroll, then, with the needle still in the fabric, lift the presser foot and insert the folded fabric into the scroll at the front.

Tips on perfect hemming

1 Insert a new needle to suit the fabric, such as size 10/70 or 12/80 for fine fabrics.

2 Getting started can be difficult as the feed dogs are only partially covered, so pin a small scrap of tearaway or soluble stabilizer underneath at the start so that the foot and feed dogs have something to work with.

3 Use a narrow rolled hemmer for very lightweight fabrics such as voile, chiffon, and handkerchief linen to make hems approximately 1⁄16–1⁄12in (2–3mm) wide and a 1⁄16in (2mm) narrow hemmer for other lightweight fabrics. For light- to medium-weight fabrics such as shirting, cottons, poly/cottons, and raw silks, use a ½–⅛in (3–4mm) narrow hemmer to make hems 1⁄12–¼in (3–6mm) wide or for poplins, flannel, and fine wool a 1⁄6–¼in (5–6mm) hemmer.

To help feed fabric evenly, add a strip of tearaway or soluble stabilizer under the fabric so that the feed dogs are completely covered.

4 To help the fabric feed evenly, roll the raw edge to the wrong side with right-hand thumb and finger, and hold the folded narrow edge up and toward the left slightly to help it feed through the scroll into a loop.

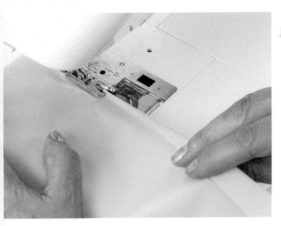

5 Continue to feed the fabric evenly, working quite slowly so that you can control how much is rolled into the foot.

Overcast foot

The overcast foot is used to neaten the fabric edges easily as it is designed to allow the thread to lap over the fabric edge, preventing them from fraying. It provides an easy way to prepare garment pieces before sewing them together as the foot is designed to hold the fabric edge flat, preventing it curling or puckering, as stitches are formed. When used with an overcast stitch, the effect is similar to the neatened edge achieved with a serger.

Janome overcast foot

WHAT AN OVERCAST FOOT LOOKS LIKE

Not all overcast feet look the same, although all have the same purpose. An overcast foot may have one or two toes, one of which is aligned with the fabric edge. It also has a pin, brush, or metal guide protruding below the foot, to prevent the fabric edge puckering or curling, making it very easy to overcast neatly. It is used with a zigzag, three-step zigzag stitch, or overcast stitch. The needle goes from side to side over the metal pin as it stitches. Use it with zigzag or three-step zigzag stitch as a clean finish, or with an overcast stitch to sew a seam and neaten the edge.

Universal overcast foot is available to fit most brands.

Use an overcast foot to attach the rib knit cuff to neck or sleeve edge

Cut the ribbing to size and join the short ends to make a continuous loop. Attach to the neck edge, right sides together, stretch the ribbing to fit as you sew with a 1/4in (6mm) seam allowance.

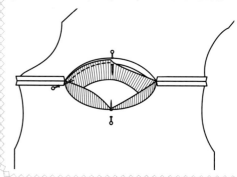

USING AN OVERCAST FOOT

Designed to sew on the edge of fabric, this is a great foot to use for quickly neatening the raw edges. Combine it with an overcast stitch and you can stitch the seam at the same time.

1 Attach the overcast foot and place the fabric edge under the foot, so the edge of the fabric butts up against the extension.

2 To neaten a raw edge of seam allowance, select a zigzag or three-step zigzag stitch. The stitches will go side to side, over the pin, brush, or metal guide.

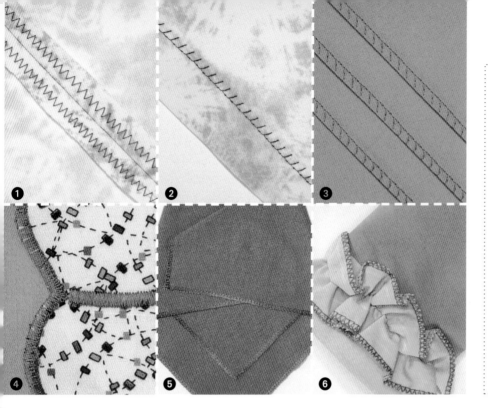

①

②

③

④

⑤

⑥

Adjustable overcast stitch foot

An adjustable overcast stitch foot is also available (also known as an adjustable blind hem foot). This has a screw on the right side which can be turned to adjust the wire or pin position, and thus the width of the seam being stitched.

IDEAS FILE

1 Prevent fabric edges rolling: Use an overcast foot when sewing stretch fabrics that have a tendency to roll or curl.

2 Hem stretch fabrics with this foot: Turn up the hem and, with wrong side uppermost, align the hem edge against the guide on the foot and stitch with an overcast stitch so that most of the stitching is on the hem allowance. From the right side, a bold decorative stitch will be visible.

3 Make stitched tucks: Fold the fabric at the required tuck position. Using a decorative thread, stitch an overcasting stitch at the folded edge.

4 Encase raw edges: Satin stitch over the edge of the fabric to completely encase the raw edge. This is useful for 3-D appliqué, napkin edges, etc.

5 Neaten edges: Use a contrast thread color and overcast stitch to edge a single layer of fabric to create a decorative finish.

6 Make decorative ruffles: Cut strips of fabric and overcast both long edges before gathering down the center to create double-edged ruffles that can be attached to the shirt front or hem.

3 Trim away any excess seam allowance. (Note: if sewing lightweight fabrics, zigzag stitch close to the seam line and then trim the seam allowance close to the zigzag stitch, or press both seam allowances together and stitch together at the same time.)

4 To stitch a seam and neaten the edge in one pass, select an overcast/over-edge stitch (which includes straight stitching and sideways stitching), and sew with a regular seam allowance.

5 When sewing with an overcast stitch that stitches the seam and neatens the edge in one pass, select a stitch to suit the fabric. One that stitches forward only is suitable for lightweight fabrics, while one that has back and forth stitches is better for medium- to heavyweight knit fabrics.

CHAPTER 3
Specialty fabric & technique feet

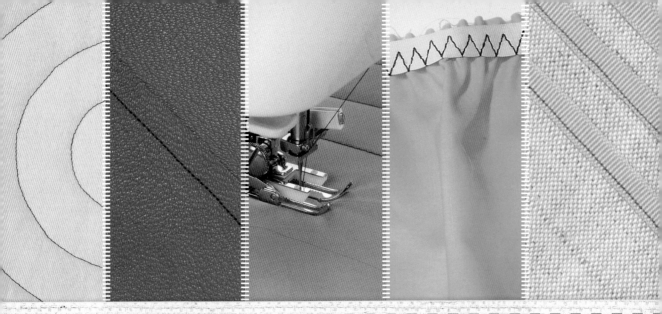

Having mastered the basic feet and techniques, it's time to move on to some specialty techniques that take your sewing to the next level. With this next group of feet you can sew sticky, slippery, and bulky fabrics with ease, such as leather, suede, and PVC silks, satins, and chiffons, as well as fleece, fur, toweling, and tartans. This chapter is about those glorious fabrics that are often avoided by beginners, but with the right feet and our simple steps, can be tackled with confidence. We even show you how to create the special seam used on jeans and hide stitching in the ditch!

Brands may vary. The Janome roller foot (top) has a long, textured barrel wheel at the front, whereas the Husqvarna (bottom) has four small smooth wheels.

Roller foot

A roller foot has one or more rolling wheels to sew fabrics that are otherwise difficult to feed under a standard presser foot. It is an ideal foot to use for thick fabrics, leather, vinyl, and jersey. It allows the fabric to move steadily under the foot without sticking, thus giving a line of even stitches.

Make a test seam first
When using a roller foot on a fabric with a delicate surface, carry out a test seam first to make sure the texture of the wheel does not mark it. If it does, place a long strip of tissue paper below the wheels and on top of the fabric to protect it.

WHAT A ROLLER FOOT LOOKS LIKE
A roller foot can be made from either metal or clear plastic. It has one or more wheels which sit between the toes and on the underside of the foot, making it glide smoothly over the fabric.

HOW A ROLLER FOOT WORKS
At the same time as the sewing-machine feed dogs move the fabric along, the textured wheels grip and roll over the surface, moving the layers smoothly together while the stitches are formed. This ensures an evenly fed seam and stitches of a consistent size with no rippling or stretching. This is essential when sewing stretchy fabrics that might otherwise ripple and extend under a standard presser foot. On leather, suede, or vinyl, where the surface may stick to the underside of the presser foot and hold it back, the roller foot glides smoothly over the surface, although occasionally the textured wheel may mark the surface of the fabric, so one with smooth wheels or a non-stick foot might be better.

ROLLER FOOT ALTERNATIVES
A roller foot is one of several feet that help to feed fabric smoothly under the needle. Alternatives include the Teflon-coated foot (see panel opposite) and the walking foot (see pages 54–57). Depending on the project, a walking foot or Teflon foot may be suitable as these also work well on stripy, stretchy, sticky, or bulky fabrics where an even feed is necessary.

Universal roller feet are available to fit most brands.

SEWING WITH A ROLLER FOOT
Use this foot when sewing thick or stretchy fabrics or for sewing materials which may be impeded by their surface texture. Here we demonstrate how easily the roller foot copes with a stretch fabric.

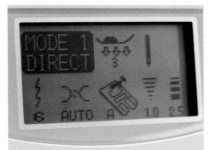

1 Attach the roller foot to the sewing machine and fit a stretch or ballpoint needle. Select an appropriate stretch stitch to sew the seam. If a pre-programed stretch stitch is not available, set a very narrow zigzag (0.5mm wide by 12spi (2mm) long).

2 With the fabrics placed right sides together, position under the needle and roller foot. Place the raw edges of the fabric to the ⅝in (1.5cm) guide line.

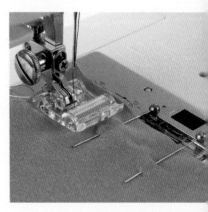

IDEAS FILE

1 Mock serged seam: Select a pre-programed overcast stitch and sew a seam with the left stitches on the seam line. Trim away the excess seam allowance, leaving the stitches right on the edge to prevent fraying. Ideal for Lycra/Spandex knits.

2 Sewing thick fabric: To sew a plain seam, fit the roller foot and lengthen the stitch to approximately 6 spi stitch length (4 mm). The foot will glide over the layers and prevent them from separating and the longer stitch will cope with the extra thickness.

3 Topstitching on leather or plastic: Use the roller foot or Teflon-coated foot to slide over the leather when topstitching. Lengthen the stitch and use a topstitch thread for the best results.

4 Matching stripes or prints: Matching stripes and bold prints is easy with the help of the roller foot. Place pins perpendicular to the seam and remove in the process of stitching to keep the pattern matching along the seam.

5 Sewing clear elastic: Whether controlling the edges on swimwear or stabilizing a shoulder seam, clear elastic or rubber is a useful product but it does tend to stick to the base of a standard presser foot. It's easy with a roller foot.

Non-stick foot

A non-stick foot, which can also be called an ultra-glide foot or Teflon-coated foot, has a smooth surface on its underside which slides easily over the fabric. This is particularly useful when sewing leather, plastic, or vinyl which might stick to the base of a standard presser foot. Use it instead of a roller foot or walking foot to achieve an even feed of fabric when sewing.

Teflon patches

These stick to the underside of a standard presser foot and work in the same way, allowing the foot to slide over the material surface.

Topstitch thread unavailable?
If a topstitch thread is not available, wind some standard thread onto a spare bobbin and feed both bobbin and reel threads through the guides and the needle. The two threads give a bolder line—more like a topstitch thread.

3 Lower the needle and foot, then sew the length of the seam, reversing over the first and last few stitches to secure the seam well at both ends.

4 The seam is smooth and flat with stitches of an even length.

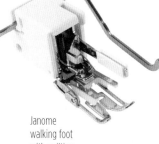

Janome walking foot with quilting guide alongside

Janome walking foot with quilting guide attached

Walking foot

The walking foot is designed to feed layers of fabric evenly. It works in conjunction with the feed dogs in the needle plate below, and moves the upper and lower layers at the same rate to prevent one shifting over the other. This ensures that at the end of sewing a seam, the fabrics remain the same length. Also called an "even feed" foot, this gadget works well when sewing multiple layers of cloth, on stretchy fabrics, and when quilting.

WHAT A WALKING FOOT LOOKS LIKE

The walking foot is a bulky attachment with a large body at the back and long parallel feet which grip the surface and walk over the fabric. A lever on the side of the foot sits over the needle bar when fitted and this controls the movement of the foot as it travels over the fabric when sewing. The bottom of the foot has ridges to grasp the fabric and move over it easily.

FITTING A WALKING FOOT

When attaching the walking foot, place the lever on the side over or around the needle bar on the sewing machine and fit the foot as normal, clipping or screwing it in place. As the bar lifts and lowers with the movement of the needle, in and out of the fabric, the foot raises and lowers at the same time.

Check the position of the side lever
If the walking mechanism does not work when fitted, check that the side lever is placed over the needle bar.

QUILTING WITH A WALKING FOOT

A walking foot is an ideal attachment to use when quilting as the multiple layers of fabric and batting/wadding are fed under the needle evenly in spite of their thickness, resulting in regular stitches. Prepare the panel for quilting and baste the fabrics together. Mark the fabric position of the quilt lines with chalk or a fade-away marking pen.

1 Fit the walking foot to the sewing machine, ensuring it is securely attached with the side lever over the needle bar. Select an appropriate needle for quilting and thread up as normal.

2 Increase the stitch length to approximately 8spi (3mm) to accommodate the thickness of the layers.

If the lever is not placed over the needle bar, this action will not occur, and the walking foot will not be able to grip the fabric as intended.

HOW A WALKING FOOT WORKS

As the needle rises and lowers, creating stitches as it goes, the lever on the side of the walking foot lifts and drops at the same rate. This movement controls the gripping feet which walk over the material rather than any other presser foot, which would slide over the fabric. This walking action, in conjunction with the feed dogs below, keeps the layers together and does not allow the upper layer to be pushed over the lower one—hence, feeding the fabric evenly as it sews.

WHEN TO USE A WALKING FOOT

A walking foot is one of the most useful attachments available. Use it for quilting or when sewing multiple layers of fabric that

Rotary even-feed foot

This gadget feeds fabric evenly using rotary caterpillar tracks rather than moving feet. It is available in a set that includes attachments for blind hemming, rolled hemming, and bias binding attachments.

Integrated walking action

Some machines have a built-in, even-feed mechanism. These machines do not have a separate foot attachment to be fitted, but the attachment is just pulled into place when required.

might otherwise shift lengthways when they are being stitched. Choose this foot when sewing fabrics with a dense pile or a surface that might stick to a standard presser foot like suede, leather, or vinyl. It is a perfect attachment to use when joining long curtain panels with a bold design as the fabric will not shift when they are being sewn, and the pattern will match along the entire length of the seams. Sewing stretch fabric with a walking foot ensures that the cloth is fed evenly, preventing any rippling that can occur with a standard presser foot.

Universal walking feet are available to fit most brands.

3 Starting with one of the central lines of quilting, place the needle over one end of the line and lower it into the fabric. Lower the walking foot into position and sew steadily along the marked line.

4 Quilt the next line, sewing in the same direction and working from the center outward toward the edges of the panel.

5 Quilt all rows, sewing in the same direction to prevent twisting and always work from the center outward.

Quilting guide

A quilting guide is a useful attachment that can be fitted to the walking foot to allow quilt lines to be regularly and evenly spaced. This simple device is a shaped metal bar which slots into a hole in the walking foot. Its position is adjusted to the size required for the spacing of the quilt lines. After the first row of stitching is sewn, the bar is positioned and placed over the first line of quilting to ensure a parallel one next to it. If this guide is used for all subsequent rows of quilting, the lines will all be equally spaced and parallel.

Lengthen the stitch when sewing velvet
When sewing velvet, as well as using a walking foot, lengthen the stitch to 8spi (3mm) to cope better with the fabric depth.

IDEAS FILE

1 Quilting: Use the walking foot to feed the thick layers of fabric and batting evenly and produce a regular stitch length.

2 Spiral quilting: The walking foot makes it easy to sew concentric circles of quilting rather than straight lines.

3 Sewing stripes, checks, or bold prints: A bold print or stripe remains matching along its entire length with the help of a walking foot. Place pins across the seam, then remove when stitching.

4 Sewing thick pile fabrics: Layers of velvet, toweling, and faux fur have a tendency to travel over each other when seaming with a standard presser foot. A walking foot feeds them evenly.

5 Suede/leather/vinyl: A standard presser foot may stick to some fabrics or animal skins. As well as fitting a walking foot, use a leather point needle, a slightly longer straight stitch, and select an appropriate seam like a lapped seam to reduce bulk.

6 Sewing fleece fabric: Fleece is a thick fabric with some stretch. Sew using a narrow zigzag stitch. A walking foot attached will cope with the depth of the layers and prevent the seams from stretching.

7 Stretch fabric: A seam sewn with a stretch fabric tends to ripple and stretch out of shape unless a walking foot is fitted to feed the fabric through evenly.

HEMMING STRETCH FABRIC WITH A WALKING FOOT

Use a walking foot to reproduce a manufactured-looking hem on a T-shirt or cotton knit top. In conjunction with a twin needle to give parallel rows of topstitching, the walking foot stitches the hem without stretching or pulling the cotton knit edge out of shape. The bobbin thread works between the two needles, producing a zigzag stitch on the wrong side. This provides an element of stretch so that the stitching moves with the fabric without breaking the thread.

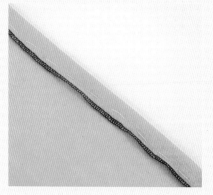

1 Neaten the raw edge of the garment (with zigzag or serging) and fold up a ³⁄₄in (2cm) hem to the wrong side. Hold the hem in place with pins or hand basting.

2 Attach the walking foot to the sewing machine, making sure the lever fits over the needle bar, and fit a twin needle (double needle) threaded with two reels of thread through the thread guides and needle eyes.

①

②

③

④

⑤

⑥

⑦

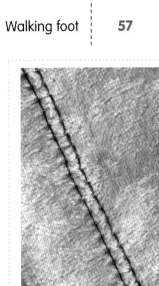

Twin needle stretch hem

Use a twin needle (double needle) on a stretch fabric to give a manufactured finish to a hem. See the step-by-step sequence below.

4 Sew parallel to the hem edge, working round the entire circumference, then pull the threads to the wrong side to fasten off. Pull the hem to check that the stitches stretch with the cloth. Press to finish.

3 With right side facing upward, position the fabric under the walking foot with the twin needles over the hem; the right needle approximately ⁵/₈in (1.5cm) from the folded edge. Lower the needles and the walking foot.

Stitch in the ditch foot

The stitch in the ditch technique is used by quilters and dressmakers to follow and sew in the join of a seam. Often used when attaching a waistband, the guide on the foot sits on the surface, in the seam, allowing the needle to produce a line of stitches directly over the seam. When completed, as the fabric rolls back into position, the stitches will be hidden in the seam.

The Husqvarna clear stitch-in-the-ditch foot (top) has a small hole for straight stitch while the Janome ditch quilting foot (bottom) has a wider hole for zigzag stitch.

WHAT A STITCH IN THE DITCH FOOT LOOKS LIKE

A vertical flange or guide sits through the middle of the foot. At the rear of this metal strip or guide is a space for the needle to enter the fabric in an ideal position for stitching. Most feet have a small hole for straight stitch only, but others can take zigzag stitching and these are more versatile. Feet vary in appearance between different manufacturers but all have a central flange as a common feature. Some are metal while others are made from clear plastic for better visibility. An adjustable foot is also available for some sewing machines with a ¼in (6mm) guide as well as the central guide for ditch stitching.

Use a zipper foot instead

If a stitch in the ditch foot is not available, try using a zipper foot tucked close to the ditch. The thick edge can be pulled to the right, allowing the needle to penetrate the ditch and form the stitches in the correct place.

HOW A STITCH IN THE DITCH FOOT WORKS

Provided the guide follows the seam, the stitching will be placed perfectly within the seam channel. Whether securing a waistband on a pair of pants or a skirt, or joining layers of a quilt, the guide is placed in the join of the seam and the needle stitches exactly in the ditch.

SEWING WITH A STITCH IN THE DITCH FOOT

Sew the waistband to the right side of the skirt/pants and pin or baste ready for stitching in the ditch.

1 Place the pins in the join of the waistband and skirt, catching the layers below it. Check the wrong side to ensure the pins hold the fabric evenly along its length.

2 Attach the stitch in the ditch foot, fit an appropriate needle for the fabric being used, and thread up the sewing machine with a suitable thread.

3 Place the fabric below the foot and position the guide directly over the seam. Lower the presser foot and then turn the handle to lower the needle onto the seam.

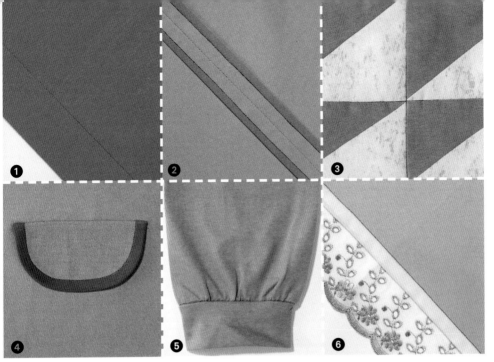

① ② ③

④ ⑤ ⑥

Try a stretch stitch with the foot
The stitch in the ditch foot has a small hole for straight stitch only. Check if a stretch stitch is possible with the foot and use for knit fabrics.

Use color-matching thread for invisible stiches
Use a good color-matching thread for stitching in the ditch so that the stitches will not be seen. In fact, a slightly darker shade will be hidden in the shadow of the ditch.

IDEAS FILE

1 Completing a band: Attach a band to the front edge of a robe or cardigan. Sew the edge of the band to the right side of the front opening, then wrap round and tuck the seam allowance under. Pin from the right side, catching the edge of the seam allowance underneath and stitch in the ditch through all the layers.

2 Finishing a seam: Cut a bias strip of fabric approximately 1in (3cm) wide and place one raw edge to the edge to be finished with right sides together. Sew a narrow ¼in (6mm) seam and trim to ⅛in (3mm). Press and wrap over the edge and stitch in the ditch to hold in place. Trim any excess on the underside.

3 Quilting patchwork: After piecing a quilt with a quarter-inch foot (see page 86), attach the layers by stitching with the foot through the seams of the patchwork.

4 Decorative binding: Attach a binding or a Hong Kong style finish to a pocket flap, stitching in the ditch to finish.

5 Finishing a cuff: Use the ditch stitch foot to complete a cuff, sewing at the join from the right side through all layers below. (Make use of the free arm to slide the cuff onto the sewing machine for ease of sewing.)

6 Attaching lace to a hem with a tuck: With right sides together, sew the lace to the hem. Press flat and wrap the lace around the hem allowance. Place the flange between the lace and hem through all the layers, then press the fold down over the top of the lace.

4 When everything is in position, gently ease the seam apart in front of the foot and sew over the seam, watching the guide rather than the needle, making sure it sits in the seam.

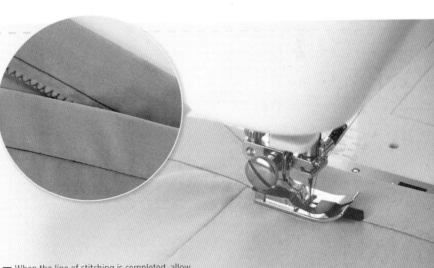

5 When the line of stitching is completed, allow the seam to roll naturally back over the surface stitching to conceal it. The layers are now joined securely but the stitches are concealed.

Flat fell foot

Flat fell seams have been sewn for years without a specially designed presser foot, but this little gadget makes it so much easier to achieve a perfectly neat finish every time. Shaped to allow the extra depth of the seam to slide under the foot easily, it ensures that a neat, straight line of topstitching is sewn in the best position for the seam.

Classic Husqvarna flat fell foot. Note the characteristic large channel on its underside.

WHAT A FLAT FELL FOOT LOOKS LIKE

A flat fell foot has a large channel on its underside to allow a depth of fabric to pass under the foot unimpeded. It has a lip on the left side to turn the fabric edge over so that it can be sewn down to the layers below. On the top, the foot sits over the folded layers and positions the seam appropriately for topstitching. Lines are marked on the foot as guides to making a perfect flat fell seam.

HOW A FLAT FELL FOOT WORKS

The guides on the foot help to feed the fabric edges in the correct positions for making a flat fell seam. Once the first line of stitching is sewn, the seam is fed in flat with the seam allowances uppermost. The foot turns the upper raw edge over and holds it in place, while the final topstitching is sewn. The shape of the foot positions the seam precisely, allowing the needle to produce perfectly positioned stitching at a regular distance from the edge consistently along its length.

Use a jeans needle to sew flat fell seams
When sewing flat fell seams on denim or other tough fabrics, use a jeans needle. The thick layers require a strong needle to penetrate the fabric.

SEWING A FLAT FELL SEAM
This is a popular seam for use on jeans and reversible clothing as it is strong with a neat finish on both right and wrong sides.

1 Attach the flat fell foot to the sewing machine and thread with topstitch thread for a bold finish. Fit a topstitch needle and place the needle in the center position. Lengthen the stitch to ⅛in (3mm). Place one piece of fabric (right side down) with its edge on the right side of the foot and the second piece over it (right side up) with the cut edge level with the guide, ¼in (6mm) to the left. Sew the seam.

2 Press the seam open with all the seam allowance to one side and the longer seam allowance over the smaller one.

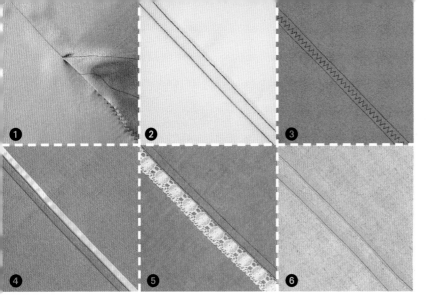

① ② ③

④ ⑤ ⑥

IDEAS FILE

1 Top and edge stitching on a lapped seam:
Create a lapped seam rather than a flat fell seam as it is less bulky. Neaten the raw edges, or use a fabric that does not ravel, and fold the top layer on the seam line. Place this over the seam line on the other piece of fabric and edge stitch the seam using the flat fell foot.

2 Traditional jeans seam: Use contrasting topstitch thread to sew a flat fell seam on denim or canvas-type cloth.

3 Decorative stitch: Make a flat fell seam but select a decorative stitch for topstitching. This makes an attractive alternative to straight stitch and looks good from both sides.

4 Flat fell seam with grosgrain ribbon: Sew the first step of a flat fell seam, then press open with the seam allowances to one side. Tuck satin or grosgrain ribbon under the flat fell seam, leaving ¼in (6mm) showing and sew with the flat fell foot in place.

5 Flat fell seam with lace: As an alternative to ribbon, tuck a length of lace under the flat fell seam before topstitching. Use the guides on the foot to turn and position the seam allowance over the lace.

6 Attaching ribbons or tapes: Use the flat fell foot to guide narrow ribbons into place and sew them to a backing fabric. Use the width of the foot to align the ribbons.

Humper jumper or Jean-a-ma-jig

These small gadgets slide under the presser foot to take up space when stitching through thick, uneven layers to allow the foot to remain level—for example, when hemming jeans and stitching over a seam. This keeps the stitches a consistent size. Without it, there is a chance that the foot will be hindered, then jump some distance, creating several small stitches followed by one large one.

3 Lightly press the upper seam allowance under for the first 1in (2.5cm) of the seam and feed this under the foot. Use the guide lines marked on the presser foot to position the seam correctly.

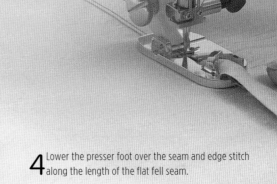

4 Lower the presser foot over the seam and edge stitch along the length of the flat fell seam.

CHAPTER 4
Pretty edges

Our next selection of feet include those that help make edges of garments and furnishings stand out from the crowd. Along with all the feet that make the job easier, we show how to add gathers, perfectly formed ruffles, neatly bound edges, elastic edging, and dramatic contrast piping. With all these techniques you can turn a simple cushion into piped perfection, a sleeveless top into a designer original, gather yards of tulle for a bridal headdress, or add ruffles to clothes or furnishings. While some of these feet look scary, follow the simple step-by-step sequences provided and you will be ruffling, gathering, piping, and binding with ease!

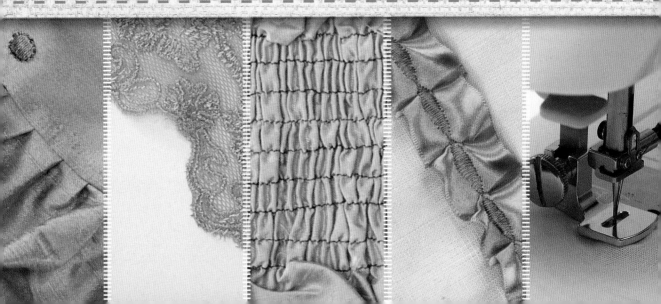

Gathering foot

This simply shaped foot makes it possible to gather a length of cloth either in a single layer or to attach it to another, gathering and stitching in one step. It allows the gathering to be created as it passes under the needle and foot rather than having to sew long rows of gathering stitches, then pulling them up evenly by hand.

Most gathering feet are made to fit any machine

Test a sample of gathering
Test a sample of gathering in the chosen fabric before sewing a project to see how much it gathers; a soft, light fabric will work better than a heavier one.

WHAT A GATHERING FOOT LOOKS LIKE
The gathering foot is small and fat. It has a chunky front or a fold of metal at the front, giving a double layer with a slot or gap on the left but enclosed on the right. It has only a single layer of metal at the back, which does not come in contact with the throat plate of the sewing machine.

HOW A GATHERING FOOT WORKS
To gather a length of cloth, feed the fabric edge under the foot and sew. The clearance at the rear of the foot allows the fabric to crinkle and gather. To attach the gathered fabric to a second layer, slot a second piece of fabric through the slot in the foot above the first layer and sew. The lower fabric will gather and attach to the upper layer, which will remain flat.

Twin needle gathering
A single row of gathers can cause a frill or gathered edge to twist, making it difficult to work with. Use a twin needle and a gathering foot for a flatter finish which will not curl up as readily, making it easier to sew it in place. Try a wide-spaced twin needle to control the edge.

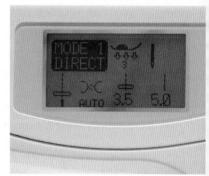

SEWING WITH A GATHERING FOOT
Use this foot to gather one piece of lightweight fabric to a second with evenly spaced tucks/gathers. Trim the raw edges smooth as a rough edge will be more difficult to feed into the gathering foot.

1 Fit the gathering foot to the sewing machine following the manufacturer's instructions. Make sure the folded edge is at the front with the slot or gap (if there is one) on the left. It is a small foot and on some models it is possible, inadvertently, for it to be attached backward.

2 Select the longest straight stitch ready for gathering. The central needle position can be used or, if preferred, place the needle on the left to increase the seam allowance on the flat layer.

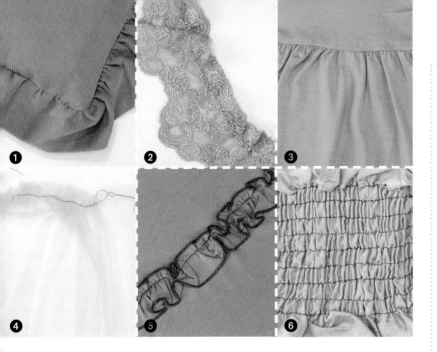

① ② ③

④ ⑤ ⑥

To encourage more gathers

To encourage more gathers, place a finger at the back of the presser foot to slow the progress of the fabric.

Using a gathering foot: practical points

1 The foot works best with soft, lightweight fabrics and has less gathering effect on medium, heavy, or stiff fabrics. The ruffle foot (see page 66) is a more versatile tool as it both gathers and ruffles all weights of cloth.

2 It is difficult to assess the final length of the gathered fabric as different fabrics gather up at different rates. Trial and error is the only way to work out how much fabric is needed to gather to a set length.

3 Due to the design of the foot, the seam allowances of the two layers being sewn are different widths. This can be awkward to handle.

IDEAS FILE

1 Cushion with frill: Attach a gathered frill to the edge of a pillow or cushion. Sew to the front of the cushion, then stitch to the back using the first line of stitches as a guide.

2 Gather lace edging: Gather a length of flat edging lace before sewing it to a garment. Sew it to a collar, cuff, or hem.

3 Gather a skirt to a yoke: Use the gathering foot to attach a skirt panel of a dress to the yoke or bodice in one step, saving precious sewing time.

4 Gather netting: Gather up layers of net to make an underskirt of a full-skirted dress or when making a ballet tutu.

5 Gather a fabric strip: Serge the edges of a strip of fabric and gather it up with a gathering foot before sewing it onto the surface of a garment.

6 Shirring with elastic: Fill the bobbin with shirring elastic and sew several parallel rows of straight stitching. This removes the need to alter the sewing-machine tension when shirring with another, standard foot.

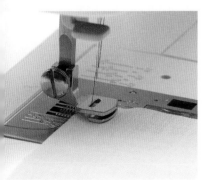

3 Place the fabric to be gathered face up, under the presser foot, with the raw edge on the right.

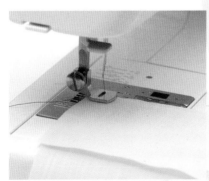

4 Slot the second, shorter length of fabric into the opening on the foot with the right side facing down and lower the needle into the fabric layers. Lower the presser foot.

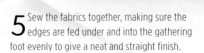

5 Sew the fabrics together, making sure the edges are fed under and into the gathering foot evenly to give a neat and straight finish.

Typical Brother
ruffle foot

Ruffle foot

A ruffle foot is more sophisticated than a gathering foot
and looks much more complicated, too. Once in place
it will gather or make regular tucks in the fabric,
producing an even ruffle along the edge. It is ideal
for sewing soft furnishings and making garments.

WHAT A RUFFLE FOOT LOOKS LIKE

This foot has a flat, horizontal lever at the
front which pushes folds of fabric under
the needle while it stitches. The number of
stitches between tucks is set with a selection
bar and the size of each tuck is regulated
with a screw.

HOW A RUFFLE FOOT WORKS

Feed the fabric in place and set the foot to
create a pleat at the desired spacing. For
example, set the foot to tuck every stitch
for gathering, or every six or 12 stitches for
further spaced pleats. The tucks or pleats
are formed when the lever at the front of
the foot pushes the fabric into place for
stitching. The size of each tuck is set with
a screw which will increase or reduce the
amount of fabric tucked by the lever.

Try a sample first
With spare fabric, try out a
sample to see how much
fabric is used to form the
ruffles required. This will make
it easier to calculate the
lengths for cutting.

**Place the needle
in the correct
position to start**
Most ruffle feet have a small
hole for the needle designed
only for straight stitching.
Make sure the needle is in the
correct position before starting
to sew.

Inserting fabric with paper
The jagged teeth on the front of
the horizontal lever which creates
the ruffles can make it difficult to
manipulate the fabric into position.
Slide the fabric edge into place
sandwiched between pieces of
paper, then slide the paper out
of the way.

SEWING WITH A RUFFLE FOOT

This is the perfect
gadget for sewing a
ruffled or gathered
edge. Here we
demonstrate how to
sew a ruffled band to
an edge to decorate a
small cushion/pillow.

1 Prepare the band for ruffling
by folding a strip of fabric in
half, lengthways, with the
wrong sides on the inside and
the raw edges level. Press flat
for a neat frill.

2 Attach the ruffle foot and
set the pleat selection to
a suitable stitch repeat to give
appropriate ruffles for the
project. Adjust the size of each
fold and select straight stitch
on the sewing machine.

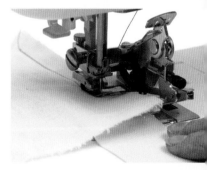

3 Feed the folded band, at an angle, into the
foot under the horizontal lever; use paper to
help (see Tip above). Place the main part of the
cushion on top with the right side facing
downward over the folded strip.

① ② ③

④ ⑤ ⑥

When turning corners

When turning corners while joining a ruffle to fabric, reduce the stitches per tuck to "one" and make three or four tucks on the corner before returning the selection bar to its original setting. This will give extra fullness round the corner.

Alternative ways of gathering

If a gathering foot or ruffle foot are not available, there are other methods of gathering. One means of doing so, especially on a heavier cloth, is to set the sewing machine to zigzag and stitch over strong narrow cord. The cord is then pulled up through the stitches. Use a zigzag foot (see page 34) or a cording foot (see page 90) for this type of gathering.

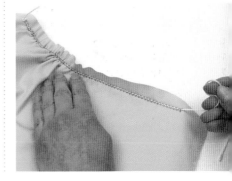

IDEAS FILE

1 Ruffle a ribbon: Ruffle a length of ribbon (set to 12 stitches per tuck) through the center and sew to the surface of fabric for a decorative finish.

2 Insert a ruffled strip: Ruffle a strip of cloth and insert it between two flat pieces of fabric for a textured effect. Six stitches per tuck were used on this project.

3 Add a frill: Create a pretty edge on a child's dress with a ruffled frill at the hem,

4 Gathered/tucked tiers: Make a skirt with several tiers of gathers or tucks using the ruffle foot.

5 Lace edge: Create a lacy edge by ruffling some cotton lace edging six or 12 stitches per tuck and sew this to the edge of a collar or cuff.

6 Gather veiling: Gather a wedding veil with a ruffle foot before adding flowers or a tiara and comb. Fold as necessary and ruffle with one stitch per tuck to give fullness.

5 When the ruffle is attached to one side, place the back of the cushion over the ruffle and front with right sides facing. Return to a standard presser foot and sew through all the layers to enclose the ruffle. Turn through and fill with a cushion pad.

4 Lower the foot and stitch along the seam line, sewing and ruffling the band in position on the edge. We have pulled the fabric back to show the ruffle. At each corner, stop with the needle lowered and presser foot raised. Hold the band straight and firm while turning the main cushion fabric. Lower the presser foot and continue.

Bias binding foot

Bias binding can be wrapped and sewn over the edge of fabric to neaten it. With the aid of a bias binding foot this becomes a much easier task, allowing the binding to be sewn in one step, with the stitches perfectly placed. It does away with the need for hand sewing and makes attaching binding much quicker.

Bias binding foot from Brother

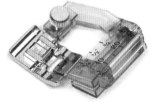

Adjustable bias binding foot from Husqvarna

WHAT A BIAS BINDING FOOT LOOKS LIKE
Most bias binding feet have a bulky slotted cone at the front of the foot to feed the bias binding into. Some feet are adjustable and take different widths of tape. Some have a movable guide so that the needle position can be adjusted for the best possible stitching line.

HOW A BIAS BINDING FOOT WORKS
The foot has a shaped guide that folds the binding into position around the edge while the central slot or space takes the main fabric edge, positioning it perfectly between the folded bias strip as it is stitched in place. The foot sews flat bias strips as well as prefolded bias to the edge of fabric. Without a bias binding foot, the

For soft furnishing projects
If you plan to sew soft furnishing projects, look for either an adjustable foot or a wider foot to take broader bindings. Narrow bindings are more appropriate for dressmaking.

process would almost definitely need to be carried out in two steps with a first line of stitching followed by folding and securing with stitching in the ditch (see page 58) or even hand hemming.

NEW ADJUSTABLE BIAS BINDING FOOT
The latest type of bias binding foot is available as a universal fitting for most sewing machines, if not for a named model. It is easier to feed prefolded

---

SEWING WITH A BIAS BINDING FOOT— PREFOLDED BIAS
Use the standard bias binding foot for a quick and easy way to bind an edge with a prefolded bias trim.

1 Sew a few stitches in the center at one end of the bias binding and leave long thread ends. These will help when feeding the bias strip into the presser foot.

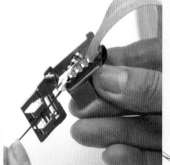

2 Before attaching the foot to the sewing machine, fold the corners of the leading edge of the bias tape to the center and pass the thread tails into a suitable slot in the presser foot.

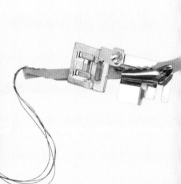

3 Pull gently to ease the tape through the presser foot, extending approximately 1in (2.5cm) beyond the exit. This will ensure the needle will sew through the tape.

binding into the foot than a standard attachment and it has an adjustable screw to position perfectly for a wide range of widths. There are two adjustable screws: one controls the width of the binding and the second sets the position of the binding in relation to the needle. These are clear plastic rather than metal for better viewing as the tape is fed through the attachment, making it much easier to sew with and achieve a good result.

Universal bias binding feet are available to fit most brands.

For cutting accurate bias strips
Use a rotary cutter, patchworker's ruler, and a self-healing mat when cutting bias strips for accuracy.

Tips on making bias strips

1 Finding the bias or true cross

Fold the straight cut edge of a length of fabric diagonally to meet the selvedge and cut along this line (45 degrees to the straight grain).

2 Cutting bias strips

Calculate the width of tape required. For a finished 1in (2.5cm) binding, cut strips of 1¾in (4.3cm). The addition is needed for seam allowances which will be tucked under. Use a rotary cutter and mat or long shears to cut smooth edged strips.

3 Joining bias strips

To make a long length of bias binding, join two or more shorter lengths together. To do this, overlap the edges by ¼in (6mm) and sew a ¼in (6mm) seam, then press the allowances open.

4 Making a continuous strip

To make a continuous strip of bias, cut diagonally across a length of fabric, from a roll, at 45 degrees. Cut a line parallel to this, creating a broad parallelogram. Mark the width of the bias required across the length and join the edges, with right sides together, to form a cylinder. Offset the end of the cylinder by the width of a strip. Sew along the seam line and cut one continuous strip of bias from the tube.

4 Fit the bias foot to the sewing. Select straight stitch and check that the needle is in the correct position. Slip the main fabric into the central slot between the folds of the binding.

5 Lower the needle and presser foot, and sew the bias binding to the fabric edge, manipulating the fabric into the guides carefully. Gently pull on the thread tails to start.

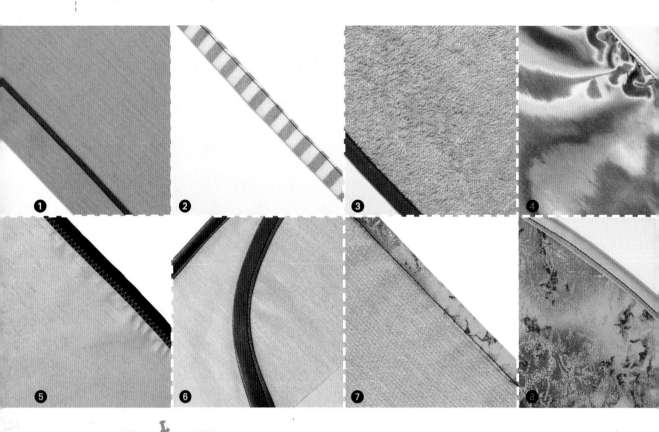

① ② ③ ④
⑤ ⑥ ⑦ ⑧

To make your own bias tape
Choose natural fabrics to make your own bias tape.
Natural fibers such as silk, cotton, or linen are easy to
press and the resulting tape will hold its shape better
than one made from a synthetic fiber.

FOLDING AND SEWING A BIAS STRIP OVER A FABRIC EDGE
Use the bias binding foot to attach the home-cut, unfolded bias strips to the edge of the fabric.

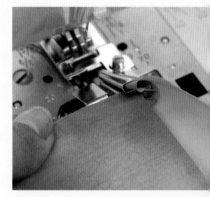

1 Cut the bias strips wider than the finished required width for binding (just under twice for the best results). Join strips if necessary to create a continuous length (see page 65).

2 Sew the end of the tape and leave the thread tails, then feed the strip into the presser foot through the large end of the foot.

3 Attach the foot to the sewing machine and slot the main fabric into the central opening between the binding edges.

IDEAS FILE

1 Narrow binding on fine fabric to neaten a hem edge: Use the binding foot to neaten the raw edge before turning up a hem.

2 Making ties: Cut straight grain strips just less than twice the required width and feed into the foot. The edges are turned under and stitched to make neat ties for various purposes. Use plain or striped fabrics for different finishes.

3 Broad binding on thick fabric: Choose a wider binding for thicker cloth such as furnishing fabric or toweling. Lengthen the stitch length to suit the thicker layers.

4 Attaching elastic to an edge: Some elastic is designed to be folded and sewn over an edge and the bias binding foot is an ideal way to attach this. Feed the elastic into the foot and place the main fabric between. Pull gently and consistently on the elastic while sewing.

5 Satin ribbon as edging: A satin ribbon will twist if applied to a curved edge but can be sewn successfully to a straight edge. A zigzag or decorative stitch works well on any bound edge rather than a straight stitch.

6 Contrast texture: Use a satin binding as a contrast on a matt fabric. Use standard ribbon, as above, on a straight edge but choose a satin bias ribbon for a curve.

7 Printed bias tape: Cut bias strips from printed cloth to make a decorative edge.

8 Shaped bound edge: Bias binding follows a curved shape without forming tucks or pleats on the edge.

Bias trim maker

Prefolded bias binding can be bought in various widths in a wide range of colors. However, making your own bias binding is made easier with the help of a bias trim maker. These are available in different sizes to make a variety of widths.

Narrow bias trim maker for ¼in (6mm) binding

⅝in (1.5cm) bias trim maker

Making folded bias strips

1 Cut strips of fabric on the true cross.
2 Feed the strip into the bias trim maker.
3 Pull the bias strip through the gadget. As this happens, the edges fold inward.
4 As the bias emerges at the opposite end, press the folded strip with an iron to help it hold its shape.

Press to keep folds in place

5 Sew the binding to the entire length, then snip and remove the remaining binding from the attachment. Check both sides of the work to ensure the raw edges are tucked under and the stitching is parallel to the folded edge.

4 Use the thread tails as an anchor and gently pull when starting to sew.

Elastic guide foot

An elastic guide foot is specially designed to sew elastic directly to the fabric. It applies the desired amount of tension to the elastic, allowing it to be sewn uniformly along its length, giving an even finish.

Elastic guide foot from Husqvarna

Test your elastic guide foot
Test your elastic guide foot on scraps of different fabric and a range of elastics to realize the possibilities of the foot. Make notes and keep these to refer back to.

Types of elastic

1 **Clear elastic:** Good for stabilizing shoulder seams and for swimwear as it does not perish.

2 **"Rubber"/elastane:** For swimwear.

3 **Knitted elastics:** Soft and stretchy; best for lightweight fabrics.

4 **Woven elastics:** Strong and thicker for heavyweight fabrics.

5 **Braided elastics:** Perfect for threading through casings as it stretches when applied directly to fabric.

6 **No-roll elastic:** Ideal for waistbands with comfortable stretch without crinkling during wear.

7 **Pretty edge elastic:** For lingerie and underwear.

8 **Cord elastics:** Range of colors makes it a good fashion choice on light and medium weights.

WHAT AN ELASTIC GUIDE FOOT LOOKS LIKE

Elastic guide feet vary in appearance but they all work in the same way. They are bulky feet with an adjustable bar or dial at the front and a guide through which to feed the elastic as it passes under the needle. Most take a range of widths of elastic and can be adjusted accordingly.

HOW AN ELASTIC GUIDE FOOT WORKS

The dial, or bar, applies pressure to the elastic to pull it as it is fed under the needle and sewn to the fabric. The pressure can be increased or reduced with the tension dial/bar to control the amount of fabric being pulled up by the elastic. An adjustable guide, in front of the needle, can be set for the width of elastic to make sure the elastic sits directly under the needle for sewing.

Universal elastic guide feet are available to fit most brands. The Elastic Wizard has a number of attachments for elastic, ribbon, and tape to fit most sewing machines.

SEWING WITH AN ELASTIC GUIDE FOOT
Models do vary but here we use Husqvarna's elastic guide foot to attach elastic.

1 Lift the roller bar at the front of the foot and feed the end of the elastic through the aperture in the base. Return the roller, pushing it back and clipping it into place.

2 Attach the foot to the sewing machine and select a three-step zigzag wide enough to cover and stabilize the elastic, preventing it from curling inward. Turn the barrel to suit the width of the elastic.

3 Adjust the tension dial at the front of the machine; the higher the number, the greater the tension and the more gathers will be achieved.

IDEAS FILE

1 Pretty edge elastic on waist of skirt or slip: Insert elastic with right side down and frilled edge to the left. Place fabric below with right side up and edges level. Stitch elastic with three-step zigzag to top edge, then fold the elastic to the wrong side and stitch again through all the layers with a standard foot.

2 Cord elastic to make a cuff: Place elasticated cord into the foot and place the sleeve below. Set to a zigzag, just wide enough to cover the cord, and stitch along the cuff line.

3 Elastane/rubber on swimwear: Neaten the edges on a swimming costume by folding the hem allowance to the wrong side. Insert the elastic and place the fabric edge with right side down and fold level with the elastic. Sew, securing the elastic to the fabric with three-step zigzag stitching.

4 Stabilize a shoulder seam on fleece fabric: Insert the elastic to the foot and set the sewing machine to a suitable overcasting seam stitch. Set the elastic tension dial to low (1 or 1.5) and sew on the seam line.

5 Hair decoration: Make pretty hair adornments or wedding garters with lengths of lace and ribbon with elastic attached through the center. Select the highest setting on the elastic tension dial.

6 Wide elastic: Use the full width of the aperture for a wider elastic and select the widest setting of three-step zigzag to hold it in place.

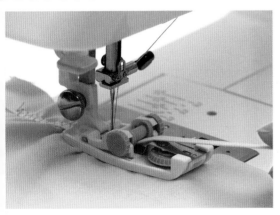

4 Place the fabric under the elastic guide foot and lower in place. Sew steadily, observing the edge of the fabric and checking that the elastic feeds correctly over the dial, into the foot, and under the needle.

5 Continue to sew the full length. To finish, lift the needle out of the fabric and elastic, raise the presser foot, and release the elastic from the tension barrel. Cut threads and elastic, leaving enough to neaten and secure the end.

Piping foot

A piping foot creates perfect piped edges. Use it for a dainty finish on an evening gown or purse, or as a heavier edge to border cushions and pillows. Use it when inserting self-covered piping made from bias strips of fabric over cord or store-bought decorative cord with a flange attached.

Clear piping foot from Husqvarna (front and back)

Use bias strips when covering piping cord
Always use bias strips when covering piping cord as the piping will be smooth and not twist around a curved or shaped edge.

Piping corners

1 Sew the piping as explained below and stop a short distance before the first corner with the needle down. Observe the point in the piping where it will reach the corner and snip in toward the cord. Continue to sew up to the snipped seam allowance and stop once again.

2 With the needle down and presser foot raised, turn the main fabric and piping round the corner. Lower the presser foot, making sure the piping sits in the groove and continue stitching.

WHAT A PIPING FOOT LOOKS LIKE

Normally plastic, to make it easier to see where the stitches are being formed, this small foot has a deep groove in its base for cord or piping to slide through when sewing. It may have a small hole for straight stitch or a larger one for zigzag stitching.

HOW A PIPING FOOT WORKS

When fitted to the sewing machine, the foot positions the piping to allow the needle to stitch very close to it. This means that when the stitching is completed, the piping sits right on the very edge like a cord. It makes a neat edge, improving the shape of, for example, a collar, cushion, or bag.

Universal piping feet are available to take various diameters of cord to fit most brands.

SEWING WITH A PIPING FOOT

Piping can be inserted into a panel of fabric or it can be enclosed and placed on an edge. Here we explain how to enclose a self-covered piping into an edge.

1 Cut a bias strip (see binding, page 69) wide enough to cover the cord with seam allowances added. Enclose the cord in the bias strip and pin along the length.

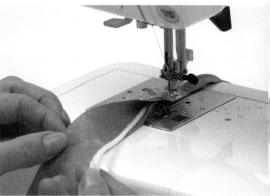

2 Fit the piping foot to the sewing machine and thread up. Set to longest straight stitch. Place the piping in the groove in the base of the foot and sew to hold it in place.

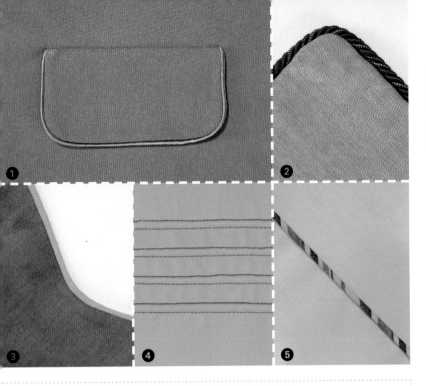

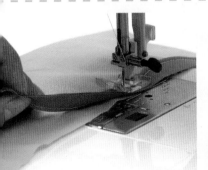

IDEAS FILE

1 Pocket flap edge: Use self-covered, fine piping to define the edges of a pocket flap. Insert the piping when sewing the front and back of the pocket flap together.

2 Using pre-made cording on a flange: Buy cording on a flange and sew into the seam when constructing a cushion. Check that the sewing-machine piping foot has a channel underneath to take the width of the cord.

3 Shaped edge at top of bodice: Add self-covered fine piping at the top edge of a bodice to define the top edge. Trim and snip into the seam allowances to make sure a flat finish is achieved.

4 Inserting cord into the fabric to add texture: To add texture to a panel, cut two layers of fabric and sew one straight line approximately 1 1/4 in (3cm) from the edge. Tuck a length of piping cord between the layers, close to the line of stitching. With the piping foot in place, trap the cord in place with a second line of sewing. Repeat parallel rows to complete the effect.

5 Contrasting piping: Piping can be made from a contrasting color or texture of fabric, or it can blend in with the design. Use a plain, printed, or striped fabric to pipe an edge or to separate and define two areas.

Use lining as an underlayer

When making self-covered piping in fine and delicate fabrics, consider using lining as an underlayer between the cording and the main fabric. This prevents the twisted structure of the cord being visible through the main fabric.

3 Place the raw edge of the piping to the main fabric with the piping sitting on the seam line. Place pins within the seam allowance to hold the piping in position for stitching. Slot the covered piping into the groove and sew the layers together.

4 To join the final layer, place it to the main fabric, sandwiching the piping in the middle with all raw edges level and matching. Pin from the previously stitched side, giving a line to follow. Reduce the stitch length to standard and sew through all layers.

5 Remove any temporary long stitches if they are visible on the right side.

CHAPTER 5
Fancy stitching

Our next selection of feet and techniques includes those that help embellish fabric, adding trims and surface texture. These feet can be used to decorate last year's outfit or add some pizzazz to plain T-shirts or cushion covers. Best of all, they can be used to turn something plain and ordinary into a wow-factor designer original. With these feet we will show how to add embellishments such as braids, beads, ribbons, and trims, how to stitch perfectly formed pin tucks, and sew simple embroidery. Get creative with free motion stitching, as well as perfectly controlled circular embroidery. All of the techniques are easily achieved—as long as you have the right foot for the job.

Brother open
toe foot

Clear view foot
variation

Open toe foot

The open toe foot gives a clear view of the area being sewn. The gap at the front of the presser foot allows precision sewing if you are following an edge or a guide line. It is ideal for appliqué and decorative stitching.

WHAT AN OPEN TOE FOOT LOOKS LIKE

Available in metal or clear plastic, the open toe foot has two long toes on either side with nothing in the middle to obstruct the view of the fabric directly in front of the needle. There is a shallow groove or channel in the base of the foot to take a build-up of decorative stitches as it glides over them.

HOW AN OPEN TOE FOOT WORKS

An open toe foot simply provides stability on either side of the working area around the needle without obscuring the view. It is therefore possible to see precisely where the needle is entering the cloth.

Universal open toe feet are available to fit most brands.

Use a tailor's awl to manipulate fabric
Use a tailor's awl to manipulate the fabric immediately in front of the needle. Fingers are too big and it would not be safe to use them so close to the needle.

IDEAS FILE
1 Decorative stitching: Use the open toe foot when sewing decorative stitching over seams of patchwork to make it easy to follow the join.
2 For bold outlines: Choose a narrow satin stitch to form the bold lines of a design and to neaten the edges of appliqué.
3 Cutwork: An open toe foot is a perfect aid when creating cutwork. It makes for easy visibility when stitching over the outline of the design with a satin stitch.

SEWING WITH AN OPEN TOE FOOT
An open toe foot is the perfect attachment when sewing decorative stitches. Here we show how to create a machine smocking effect, but the open-toe foot works equally well on a flat surface.

1 Prepare the fabric for smocking by sewing rows of gathering and pull it up into tiny tucks. Support with an iron-on tear-away stabilizer on the wrong side.

2 Fit the open toe foot to the sewing machine and thread up with appropriate thread. For a bolder finish, use two reels threaded through the guides and needle.

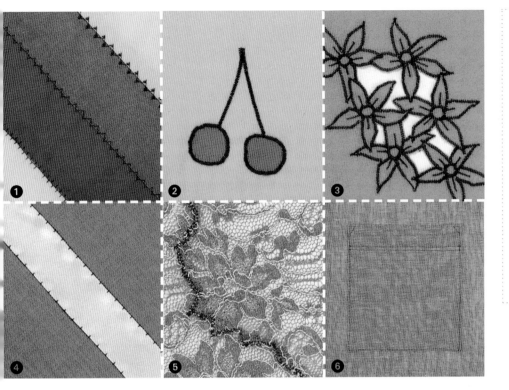

Button sewing
Although there is a presser foot specifically designed for sewing buttons in place, the open toe foot can be used for this function too. The clear area at the front of the foot holds the button securely for stitching. For full instructions, see page 42.

4 Attaching ribbon: Select an open toe foot when sewing ribbon to a backing fabric. The foot holds the work in place and allows a good view of the needle and ribbon edge being stitched. Choose an appropriate pre-programmed stitch from those available on the sewing machine.

5 Sewing lace: To maintain the pattern in lace, pieces are often lapped, with one placed over the other. They are then zigzagged together along the upper edge of the lace design to join them. The excess seam allowances are then cut away. An open toe foot makes this process much easier.

6 Topstitching: When topstitching or edge stitching on the surface of a garment, an open toe foot makes it easy to see exactly where the needle is penetrating the fabric.

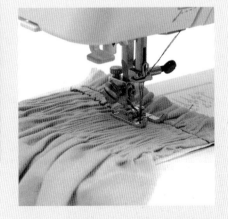

3 Select some appropriate decorative stitches. Check the sewing machine manual for typical examples of smocking stitches or try several on spare fabric to see what they look like.

4 Sew parallel rows of decorative stitches across the gathered tucks. Use the edge of the open toe foot to gauge the distance between the rows to keep them evenly spaced.

5 When the rows of smocking stitches are completed, remove the stabilizer from the wrong side and use the prepared panel as required. Panels of smocking are ideal for cushions, pillows, bags, or babies' clothing.

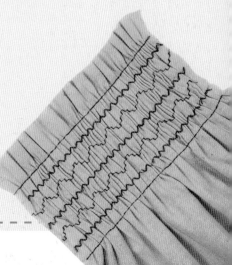

Janome darning foot

Darning/embroidery foot

Computerized embroidery machines use a special sprung foot and, while the machine moves the fabric (in a hoop), the needle rises and lowers to form the stitches as programmed. Similar feet are used on a standard sewing machine and the fabric is moved manually to create stitches. This allows embroidery, darning, and free-motion quilting to be carried out.

WHAT A DARNING/EMBROIDERY FOOT LOOKS LIKE
Long and slim, normally screwed to the arm rather than clipped to the ankle, a darning/embroidery foot often has a spring. The needle is protected by a ring, open toe, or saucer-like base and these are generally clear plastic or very small to allow good viewing of the stitch area.

HOW A DARNING/EMBROIDERY FOOT WORKS
The foot, even when lowered, will normally hover over the fabric rather than clamping it in place. As the needle lowers and penetrates the fabric, the foot engages to let the tension make a stitch. The tension is released as the needle rises, permitting the fabric to be moved and the thread to be released before the next stitch is formed.

Secure the threads
When starting to quilt, sew three stitches on the spot to secure the threads so they will not unravel. Repeat at the end of the work.

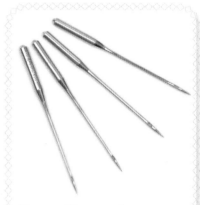

Use a quilting needle
Quilting needles have a sharp point and a narrow tapered shaft to sew through several layers

FREE-MOTION QUILTING
One of the most common uses for a darning foot is for free-motion quilting as the last stage of finishing patchwork projects.

1 Prepare the fabric for quilting with a layer of wadding/batting sandwiched between the top fabric and backing. Secure with safety pins or basting to hold the layers together.

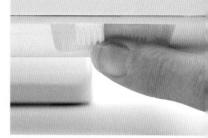

2 Lower the feed dogs to stop the fabric from being moved from front to back as it is for standard stitching. There will be a switch or lever at the back or side of the machine. Check the manual for details.

Darning, embroidery, and free-motion feet

These similar but differing feet are designed to suit particular tasks.

Free-motion quilting foot

This has no arm to fit over the needle bar, resulting in quieter stitching.

Convertible free-motion quilting foot set

This is a standard free-motion foot with three interchangeable feet, offering more convenience to suit different projects.

Echo quilt foot

This circular guide marks the distance from the needle, no matter which direction the fabric is being moved.

Tips for free-motion embroidery

■ Keep a pair of scissors with short, curved blades to hand to snip off thread ends from the surface of your work.

■ Use a firm stabilizer on the wrong side to prevent puckering and skipped stitches.

■ Place the work in a hoop to keep the design taut and flat, but make sure the fabric is not stretched and the grain is straight.

■ If necessary, reduce the needle tension slightly to prevent the bobbin thread coming into view.

■ Choose a variety of types of thread (rayon, silk, polyester, cotton, and variegated floss) to achieve a range of effects. See pages 82–83 for more on free motion embroidery.

3 Fit a darning/free-motion foot. Fill a bobbin and thread up as required. Set the needle to the center position.

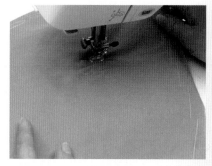

4 Consider the route of the needle before starting to sew to get a good flowing stippling stitch. Move the fabric at the same time as depressing the foot pedal. The faster the speed, the quicker the stitches will be formed; the more the fabric is moved, the longer the stitches will be. Move steadily to make consistently sized stitches.

5 Continue to move the quilt, creating continuous stippling stitches to bond the layers together.

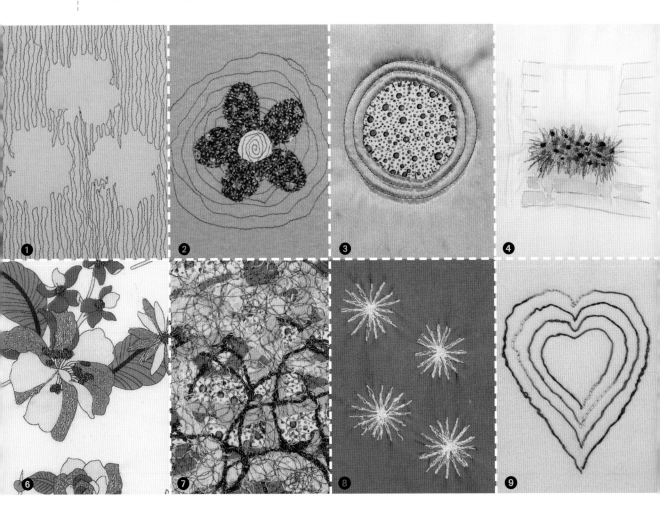

THREAD PAINTING

Free-motion machining with colored threads is a form of painting. The needle becomes the paintbrush that applies the color to the background.

1 Lightly draw the outline of a design on plain fabric. Use silk paints to add a wash of color if necessary or use threads to create all the color.

2 Stabilize the fabric on the wrong side and place it in a hoop to support the backing.

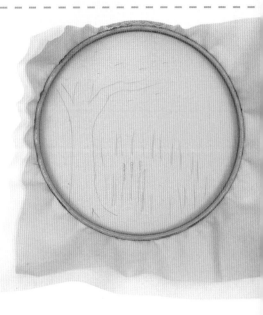

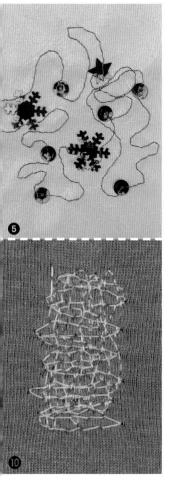

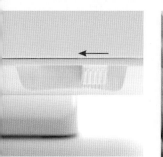

IDEAS FILE

1 Negative quilting: Pin or baste a paper template (a flower or leaf perhaps) to areas of fabric and quilt lines free-hand across the design, avoiding the paper templates. When completed, remove the paper shapes to reveal areas of unstitched fabric, giving an attractive negative effect.

2 Quick appliqué: Place appliqué pieces on the surface of the fabric and free-hand stitch over them to hold them down. Move the fabric with a haphazard motion or spiral outward from the center.

3 Echo quilting: Follow the line of an appliqué edge with rows of quilting to resemble waves. An echo foot makes it easier to follow an edge accurately.

4 Textured detail: Paint a background on fabric and pick up an area for some detail. Here there is a faint outline of a wall and window with freehand embroidered flowers in the window box sewn with a zigzag setting to create solid shapes rather than lines.

5 Sewing sequins: Attach sequins with freehand machining. Stop when a sequin is to be added and slowly lower the needle through the hole two or three times to secure, then continue to move the fabric and sew.

6 Thread highlights: Pick a printed fabric and highlight parts of the design with freehand machine embroidery. Set the stitch to straight stitch and lower the feed dogs, then fill the chosen area as if painting with a brush.

7 Making new fabric: Sandwich cut pieces of different fabrics and threads between two pieces of dissolvable stabilizer and baste the layers together. Drop the feed dogs and use freehand machine embroidery over the entire area. When the layers are stitched well together, wash away the stabilizer to achieve a new fabric and use for a small purse or a useful bag.

8 Daisies: Make daisies to decorate a plain fabric. Set the stitch to zigzag and drop the feed dogs into the machine. Stitch freehand petals in white by moving the fabric from side to side, then finish with yellow in the center, spiraling with straight stitch. Sew a row of flowers to form a border or group together in clusters over a wider area of fabric.

9 Reverse sewing: Fill the bobbin with a thick thread and place standard thread through the guides and into the needle above. Drop the feed dogs and sew with the fabric upside down. Draw an outline on the wrong side to follow.

10 Darning: Repairing a hole or worn area of cloth is easy with a darning foot. Choose a good color matching thread and move the fabric across and up and down over the area to be repaired. It is helpful to place a small patch behind on the wrong side to support the area.

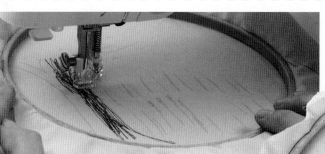

3 Drop the feed dogs and fit a darning/free-motion foot to the sewing machine.

4 With suitable thread, move the hoop while sewing to add color to the picture or landscape.

5 Build up the picture or landscape with all the colors necessary, moving the hoop to produce the stitch detail required.

Fringing/tailor tack foot

The fringing foot is also known as a tailor tack foot as it was originally designed to make tailor's tacks quickly and easily. It is used in combination with a sideways stitch such as zigzag to form loose stitches.

Janome fringing foot

Secure your work
If the fabric puckers when creating the loopy stitches, place a layer of tearaway stabilizer under the work to secure the fabric.

Use different widths of stitches

Sewing with a fringing foot provides the opportunity to create some interesting surface detail on an otherwise plain fabric. It is worth experimenting with different stitch widths to create different size loopy stitches. It is also necessary to adjust the top tension to suit the fabric. Tension set at 0 or 1 will give very loose stitches, but might cause the fabric to pucker, so back the work with a tearaway or soluble stabilizer before stitching.

WHAT A FRINGING FOOT LOOKS LIKE

The fringing foot has a raised metal bar in the center front, over which the zigzag stitches are formed so that when the work is removed, the stitches on the surface of the fabric are loose. The needle aperture is wide to accommodate the sideways stitching. Always remove the work by pulling it out from behind the needle so that the stitches don't get caught on the raised bar.

HOW A FRINGING FOOT WORKS

Using a zigzag stitch, the needle swings from side to side, forming the stitches over the protruding raised bar, thus creating loose stitches as the top thread is held away from the fabric. As well as the practical application of making tailor's tacks, it can be used creatively to add surface texture such as fringing, loop embroidery, and fagoting. Reducing the top tension to zero will help make the stitch loops bigger and prevent the fabric from puckering.

SEWING WITH A FRINGING FOOT

This foot is fun to use for a creative surface texture. One of the prettiest applications is fringing. Use contrasting thread color to make sure it stands out from the base fabric. Use fringing to decorate a hemline and pocket opening.

1 Reduce the top tension to 1 or 0 (which helps produce larger loopy stitches) and select a zigzag stitch set at maximum width. Turn the balance wheel by hand to take a couple of stitches, ensuring the needle swings side to side over the bar without hitting it.

2 Reduce stitch length to 0.35 so that the stitches are formed close together. Sew slowly, along a marked line. The loopy stitches will fall off the back of the raised bar as you stitch.

Use thicker thread to create a thicker fringe

Use a thicker thread, such as topstitch thread, or two reels through the needle to create a thicker fringe.

IDEAS FILE

1 Make tailor's tacks with a fringing foot: Set to widest zigzag stitch and sew four to five stitches. Carefully remove from machine by pulling the fabric away from behind the needle so the stitches slide off the raised bar. Once the thread loops are formed, slightly pull the fabric layers apart and cut the thread between the layers so that some of the thread marking remains in each fabric piece.

2 Stitch loop embroidery: Similar to fringing, loop embroidery is a surface decoration formed by the loopy stitches created over the raised bar of the fringing foot. Mark a simple design on the surface of the fabric and, using a contrast or decorative thread, stitch over the marked line. The stitches remain uncut and are purely for decorative interest.

3 Fagoting: Neaten the raw edges of the two sides to be joined with an overcast stitch or zigzag stitch, then fold seam allowances to the wrong side and press. Hold the two folded edges either side of the raised bar on the fringing foot about ⅙in (4mm) apart and, using a zigzag stitch set at

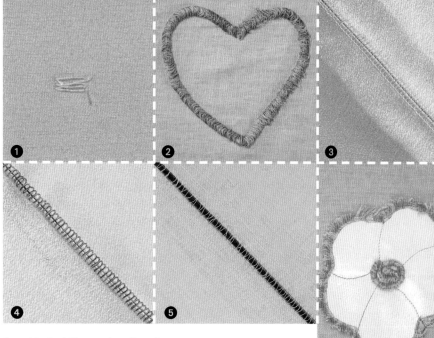

the widest width, sew together. Once pressed, pull gently apart to reveal the ladder stitching.

4 Make a feature of seams: Use two reels of contrast thread through the needle and ladder stitch two adjoining edges together.

5 Add ribbon weaving: Weave a fine, narrow ribbon through the ladder stitching.

6 Create a 3-D picture: Give a 3-D look to an appliqué flower by stitching around the edges with narrow fringing, setting the stitch width to 3.

3 Press stitches down to one side, using a press cloth to protect the thread and base cloth. Using a regular zigzag or straight stitch foot, sew down one edge of the loopy stitching to anchor the threads, using a straight stitch or reinforced straight stitch (or use a twin needle).

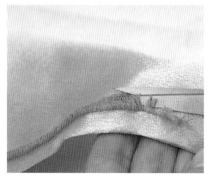

4 Working from the back of the work, cut through the loopy threads, close to the straight stitching.

5 Once the threads are cut at the back, pull the threads through to the front to form the fringing. If some loops pull through, cut through the loops too.

Edge stitch foot

There are variations of edge stitch and edging feet, but no matter what the manufacturers call them— quarter-inch foot, edge or edging foot, piecing or edge joining—they are used to sew evenly and close to the edge of the fabric or to join the edges side by side.

Husqvarna Viking edge/joining stitch foot

Trim seam allowances where seams converge
Where seams converge, at cross-sections or bulky seams, trim seam allowances to a scant ⅛in (3mm).

Border guide foot
Another foot with a similar job as an edge stitch foot is the Border Guide foot from Janome. It is a wide, clear foot with red markings. Two sets of vertical red lines allow perfect spacing of decorative rows, while the horizontal red line matches the needle drop, allowing you to accurately line up the start of each new row of stitching.

WHAT AN EDGE/PIECING FOOT LOOKS LIKE
There are two distinct variations of an edge stitch foot. One has markings (usually red) on the toes of the foot, which are spaced ¼in (6mm) and ⅛in (3mm) from the needle for accurate pivoting when reaching the end of a seam. The right side edge of the foot is also ¼in (6mm) from the center needle position, so when the fabric is placed along the edge of the foot, the seam will be ¼in (6mm) away. It may also have a thin metal guide along the right edge. The other variation has a thin metal guide in the center of the foot, protruding vertically just below the sole of the foot against which fabric can be placed.

The Universal "little" foot/edge foot is available to fit most brands.

SEWING WITH AN EDGE STITCH FOOT
This foot is particularly useful for quilting and piecing fabrics accurately, where even a slight variation in seam widths might potentially spoil the patchwork quilting effect.

1 Attach the foot and select the center needle position.

2 Position the fabric under the foot so that the edges of the fabric butt up against the right-side edge of the foot.

3 Stitch with the needle in the center position so that the stitching is exactly ¼in (6mm) from the fabric edge.

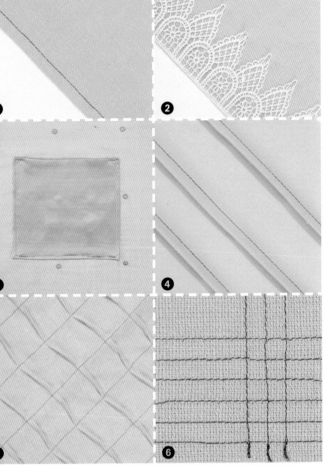

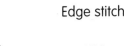

IDEAS FILE

1 Use this foot for topstitching: Butt the fabric edge up against the metal guide on the foot, and topstitch the fabric near to the edge. This is a neat finish for collars, cuffs, etc. and helps to hold the facings in place.

2 Attach lace edging: Fold the raw edge of the fabric to the inside and press. Place the fold of the fabric against the metal guide on the foot or the right edge and place a lace trim on top, also butted against the right edge/metal guide. Feeding both carefully, stitch the two edges together. The lace will sit on the fabric, right up against the edge, or the seam can be turned to the inside so the lace is protruding over the edge.

3 Attach patch pockets: Attach patch pockets in place. Butt the edge of the pocket against the right side of the foot and sew, with the needle moved to the right, close to the edge. Sew the sides and across the bottom of the pocket.

4 Make narrow tucks: Fold the fabric, wrong sides together, and butt the fold against the metal guide on the foot. With the needle set in the center position, stitch a seam. Open out the fabric and press the tuck down to one side.

5 Create twisted tucks: Having sewn a series of tucks, press all in one direction and sew horizontally across the tucks with straight stitch. Press the tucks in the opposite direction and again sew across them horizontally, about 1–2in (2.5–5cm) away from the previous stitching. Repeat along the length of the tucks, pressing alternate ways each time.

6 Parallel stitching: Use the guide on the foot to create parallel rows of topstitching. Start the first with the fabric edge against the metal guide or the right edge of the foot. Move the fabric so the guide will run along the previous stitching for the next row. Continue moving the fabric across.

5 Press the seam allowances to one side, preferably toward the darker fabric, if applicable, to minimize any show-through.

6 Join strips together, again taking care to stitch a perfect 1/4in (6mm) seam. Press the seam allowances away from each other.

4 To ensure the next corresponding seam is also exactly 1/4in (6mm), stop when the first red mark is 1/4in (6mm) from the lower fabric edge. Continue joining the pieces into a strip.

Husqvarna Viking
5-groove pin-tuck foot

Janome 5-groove
pin-tuck foot

Underside of Janome
5-groove pin-tuck foot

Pin-tuck foot

Pin-tuck feet are designed to create fine tucks quickly and easily. They are used in conjunction with a twin needle, which stitches parallel rows of stitching either side of the tuck. Pin tucks are generally associated with heirloom sewing, christening gowns, bed linen, and classic shirts.

Avoid tangled threads
Avoid top threads tangling by placing one clockwise on spindle and the other counterclockwise.

WHAT A PIN-TUCK FOOT LOOKS LIKE
The front of the foot has a small hole for straight stitching and the underside has tunnels or grooves. You can get three-, five-, or seven-groove pin-tuck feet which means you can sew rows of evenly spaced, perfectly formed pin-tucks on different weights of fabric.

HOW THE FOOT AND NEEDLE COMBINATION WORK
The twin needles use two top threads and stitch either side of the center groove so that the single bobbin thread zigzags between the top threads underneath, pulling up a little to form a raised tuck in the fabric that feeds through the groove. When the first tuck is finished, move it into the groove next to the stitching hole and start again for the next one. You can then stitch a row of perfectly formed, evenly-spaced tucks.

Needle choice
Use a twin needle with a narrow gap between the needles for fine fabrics and a wider gap for heavier fabrics (see page 23). For instance a 1/16in (1.6mm) gap and 10/70 needle is perfect for lightweight fabrics while a 1/8in (4mm) gap and 14/90 is better suited to wools. If sewing jersey, use a ballpoint or stretch needle.

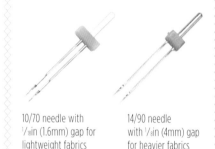

10/70 needle with
1/16in (1.6mm) gap for
lightweight fabrics

14/90 needle
with 1/8in (4mm) gap
for heavier fabrics

SEWING PIN TUCKS
If tucks are to be stitched on garment sections, do so before cutting out the piece as the tucks will reduce the width of the fabric section. Each tuck takes approx 1/4in (6mm) of fabric depending on the fabric thickness and whether tucks are regular or raised (which takes up more fabric). Thus a row of seven tucks will reduce the width by at least 1½in (4cm).

1 Attach pin-tuck foot and change needle to a twin needle. Select center needle position. Increase tension to approximately 7.

2 Feed two reels of thread through the top thread path (putting one on the second thread holder or bobbin spindle). Use the same thread in the bobbin. (Usually the same color will be used in all three spools.)

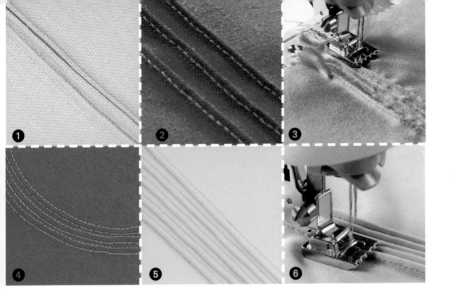

① ② ③

④ ⑤ ⑥

RAISED PIN-TUCKS

These are more pronounced and firmer than regular pin-tucks because a length of fine cord is fed under the presser foot in the center groove as the tuck is stitched. If available, use a cord guide clipped to the front of the throat plate (shown right) to keep the cord in the right place; otherwise guide it by hand as you sew.

Start with the cord in position, with at least 2in (5cm) protruding from the back of the foot. Place fabric under foot and sew the first tuck, gently guiding the cord and fabric from the front. At the end of the tuck, cut off the remaining cord before removing work from the sewing machine.

IDEAS FILE

1 Close tucks: Leave a groove between tucks, or use the presser foot edge as a spacing guide.

2 Spaced tucks: Get wider spaces using the whole pin-tuck foot as a guide.

3 Pronounced tucks: Sew cord inside the tucks (see right).

4 Curved tucks: Take care when fabric is on the bias (most stretchy part) so that it doesn't twist.

5 Imitate piping: Stretch fabric with cord filling makes rounded tucks.

6 Stretch-fabric tucks: Remember to use a ballpoint twin needle.

Attachments for raised tucks with cord

Some manufacturers include a separate throat plate or guide to direct cords through the grooves of the pin-tuck plate in order to create more pronounced and firmer pin-tucks. Janome have a plate with guide attached that is used instead of the standard throat-plate cover.

The cord is fed through a guide in front of the needles and presser foot, keeping it in line with the central groove. Husqvarna Viking has a raised-seam foot with separate guide for cords that is attached to the front of the throat plate.

3 Mark the position of the first tuck by drawing a line with a chalk pencil.

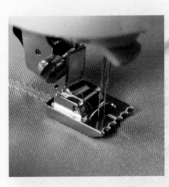

4 Follow your guide line to stitch the first tuck onto the fabric. Move the fabric so the first tuck sits in a groove right or left of center and stitch the next tuck (shown right).

Janome cording foot

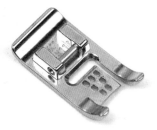

Husqvarna cording foot

Push the sewing machine back
Push the sewing machine back so the reels of cord sit in front comfortably with room for the threads to unroll as you sew.

Cording and gimping foot

Cording and gimping feet are used to add evenly spaced lines of fine yarns to the surface of the base fabric for decorative embellishment. This technique is known as couching. Between one and seven yarns can be couched in placed at one time.

WHAT CORDING AND GIMPING FEET LOOK LIKE

Cording feet have one, three, or five holes in the base of the foot or a shaped metal clip with three tunnels through which the cord is fed. They will also have a wide needle aperture to allow wide sideways stitching and a slight indentation on the underside so the cords/yarns can be smoothly stitched over.

Gimping is another term for cording or couching, but it refers specifically to couching down just one thread to create a dimensional satin stitch trim. A specific gimping foot may have just one hole through which a cord is fed.

HOW CORDING AND GIMPING FEET WORK

On the foot with holes, the cording is fed from the front to the back, through the holes from the top to the underside, with tail ends pulled to the back. There may be three, five, or seven holes to allow you to couch down up to seven yarns. If you are not using the complete number of holes available, insert the yarn into the center holes only. For the foot with the metal clip, insert the yarns from the right, again from the front to the back of the foot, clipping them into each groove or tunnel and then under the foot through the needle aperture. To couch one thread only, use the center groove.

SEWING WITH A CORDING FOOT
This is a very easy foot to use to create stunning decorative surface detailing. By combining different yarns or cords and zigzag stitch, you can add a new dimension to your work with the yarns evenly fed through the foot.

1 Feed the cording into the foot, from front to back, going from the top to the underside so the yarns are under the foot toward the back.

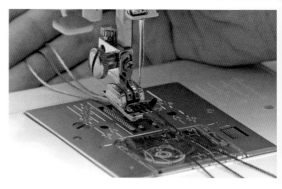

2 Place the yarn reels in front of the sewing machine. When you attach the foot make sure you hold the tail ends of the yarns toward the back.

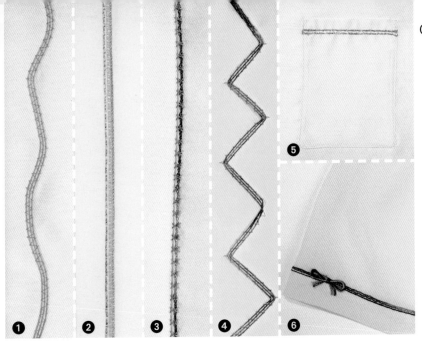

① ② ③ ④ ⑤ ⑥

IDEAS FILE

1 Choose coordinating thread: Stitch down with thread to match the most prominent yarn color so the couched yarns really stand out.

2 Use an invisible thread: This will couch the yarns in place so that the stitching is invisible. This is a great way to decorate cuffs or hemlines.

3 A decorative stitch adds another dimension: Use a decorative sideways stitch combined with bold thread color to add another dimension to the visual impact of the couching.

4 "Paint" with couched yarns: Mark a placement line to follow and create wavy patterns and shapes.

5 Add decoration to pockets: Couch down two lengths of gold braid around collars, cuffs, or onto pocket tops before attaching the pocket to the garment. Use gold thread to couch too so that the stitching is barely visible.

6 Add couched cording to hemline: Do this about 1in (2.5cm) above hem edge. Not only does this add a decorative finish, but it is perfect for children's clothes where hems are lowered as it can conceal creases or fading.

Gimping/braiding guide
Use a gimping or braiding guide to help guide the cords in front of the foot. The guide is attached through a hole in the top of the presser foot ankle and protrudes to the front which has a coil or loop, through which the cords can be fed.

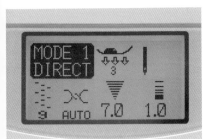

3 Next, position the fabric to be embellished under the foot and yarns and lower the presser foot. Select a three-step zigzag stitch and increase the width so that it will stitch over all of the yarns to be couched as well as stitching into the center yarns. Choose a width of about 1/4in (5–7mm) so that it just catches the outside yarns on either side.

4 Help feed the yarns in the front as you stitch. Note they will separate and evenly space themselves as they go through the grooves or holes in the presser foot.

5 For soft, rounded corners, stop with the needle down on inside of the corner (to the left), raise the presser foot and pivot the work and yarns away from you. Continue to sew. For crisper corners, stop with the needle down on the outside of the corner (to the right), raise the presser foot and pivot the work away from you.

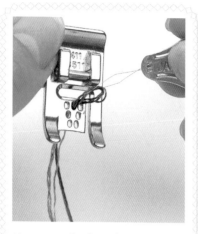

Use a needle threader to pull yarns through

Thread yarn through the grooves or holes of the presser foot before attaching the foot to the sewing machine. For a foot with holes, use a wire needle threader.

Back your work

Back work with interfacing or tearaway stabilizer when using concentrated stitches.

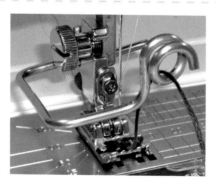

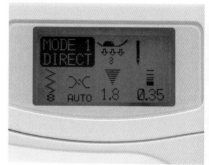

SEWING WITH ONE CORD OR "GIMPING"

Use the gimping foot to attach a fine cord, adding surface interest to a plain fabric. When combined with the braiding guide, you can really "paint" with the cord and create truly stunning results.

1 Attach the gimping foot and feed the cord down through the hole at the front and under the foot at the back. Attach the gimping/braiding guide and lay the cord through it before resting the reel in front of the sewing machine.

2 Select a zigzag stitch and adjust the width and length. Reduce the width to between 1.8 and 2 so that it stitches close to the cord on both sides, and the length to between 0.35 and 0.5 so the stitches are close together, completely covering the cord.

IDEAS FILE

1 Add a "military" look: Embellish cuffs and collars by couching rows of cord, covered with gold thread satin stitch. Note: Use the right edge of the foot as a guide for the left row of cord and then draw a guideline between the first two for the center row.

2 Create a surface texture: Turn a plain cotton top into something a little special by adding a raised surface grid made up of coached cord in the same color as the base color.

3 Gimp cord in a flowing pattern: Draw a flowing curved design on the fabric and couch a cord down following the lines to create a soutache embroidery feel (curvy, continuous thread that doesn't cross over at any point). Make sure you use the gimping guide to feed the cord. Stitch slowly and turn the work as you sew.

4 Stitch over hand-drawn patterns: Draw pretty flower shapes onto the cloth and couch the cord over the lines to add a decorative surface detail to specific areas of a plain garment or patchwork quilt.

Hold the fabric flat
Hold the fabric flat either side of the foot and guide it firmly. Satin or slippery fabrics can turn easily.

Use a stabilizer
When using a satin stitch to cover cord, back light- and medium-weight fabrics with a stabilizer so they don't pucker and use bobbin fill in the bobbin which is a lighter weight thread.

Different cords that can be used
A cording or gimping foot is used with fine yarns, thin cord, elastic thread, or crochet thread. This can be covered with widely spaced zigzag stitching so the cords are visible and provide the decorative pattern, or can be concealed beneath a close zigzag stitch/satin stitch for a raised surface treatment. Thicker yarns, braids, and beading are attached using a different type of foot (see overleaf).

3 Stitch over the cording, working slowly. Adjust the width or length of stitch again, if needed.

4 To stitch around a curve, stop with the needle down on the right side for outer curves, raise the presser foot, and pivot the work toward the right and back.

5 For an inner curve, stop with the needle down in the left, raise the presser foot, and pivot the work toward the left and back.

Husqvarna
braiding foot

Janome
beading foot

Husqvarna
Viking ribbon
foot (set of 3)

Beading and braiding foot

Bold, contrasting ribbons, beads, sequins, and thick cords stitched to the surface of a fabric can add a decorative finish that turns simple into stunning. These feet have either deep grooves to glide over the bulky trim or slots to feed flat trims through.

Weight of the beading to weight of the fabric
Make sure the weight of the beading or braid is in keeping with the weight of the main fabric. Use lightweight trims on lightweight fabric and heavier braids on coatings, furnishings, etc.

WHAT BEADING AND BRAIDING FEET LOOK LIKE
Beading feet have a deep groove on the underside. They are short, chunky-looking feet and may come in packs of two to cater for the different thicknesses of beading. Braiding, ribbon, and sequin feet have a slot at the front of the foot through which flat braid is fed. Again, they may come in packs with different widths slots, or have an adjustable screw to one side.

HOW BEADING AND BRAIDING FEET WORK
The strung beads are laid under the foot to glide easily through the groove. Feet with the smaller groove will take up to $1/12$in (2mm) diameter beads, while the deeper groove can cope with beads from $1/10$in (2.5mm) to $1/6$in (4mm) in diameter. They are attached to the fabric with a zigzag stitch that sews side to side over the beading as it is fed through. Braids, ribbons, and strung sequins are fed through the front slot of the braiding/ribbon sequin foot, before passing under the foot to the back. Stitching is then formed either over the braid with a zigzag stitch, or along the braid using a decorative stitch pattern. The width of the braid that can be used will depend on the individual manufacturer's braiding/ribbon foot.

SEWING WITH A BEADING OR BRAIDING FOOT
Using a beading foot or braiding foot to attach strings of beads, sequins, or flat trims is a quick and easy way to add distinctive embellishment. Such trims are popular on bridal wear, evening wear, and craft projects.

1 Determine which beading foot to use by pulling the strung beads through the groove on the underside of the foot. They should glide smoothly but not be too loose as they need to be kept in line so that the needle will stitch side to side without hitting the beads.

2 Attach the most suitable foot and once the fabric is in position under the foot, lay the beads under the groove. Lower the foot to hold the beads in place.

3 Select a zigzag stitch and adjust the width so that the needle just clears the beads, stitching either side. Increase the length to approximately $1/8$in (3mm). Use a thread to match the beads or an invisible thread.

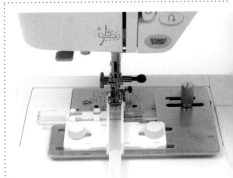

Ribbon sewing guide

Janome also have a ribbon sewing guide that can be used to make original ribbons by adding decorative stitching or even lettering. The guide is attached to the throat plate and has a slot through which ribbon is fed ready to be stitched and embellished.

IDEAS FILE

1 Adding sequins: Attach a length of strung sequins using the braiding foot and a zigzag stitch in clear thread, slightly wider than the trim. Once sewn, push the stitching between the sequins to completely conceal it. Make sure the sequins overlap away from the presser foot so they feed smoothly.

2 Layering two trims: Feed wide and narrow flat ribbons through the braiding foot and then stitch both down together with a triple zigzag stitch.

3 Create your own trims: Use a wide ribbon or braid as the base, then feed a slightly narrower one through the braiding foot and stitch in place. Top with a fine, narrow ribbon, or trim and stitch with a decorative stitch in contrast thread.

4 Couch a bulky cord in place: Use the larger groove beading foot to attach chunky cord. Either satin stitch in place (close zigzag) or simply zigzag stitch with a contrast color.

5 Attach piping with the beading foot: Fold piping cord into a strip of bias cut fabric, then place the piping on the right side of main fabric with piping running through the groove. Stitch to the left to secure in place.

6 Decorative thread and stitch over trim: Use a decorative stitch and contrast thread to attach the bulky trim, adding another dimension to the overall look of the embellishment.

Prevent the fabric from puckering
Stabilize the back of the main fabric with a suitable weight tearaway or soluble stabilizer to prevent the fabric from puckering as the trim is stitched in place.

4 Once the beading is attached, remove the work from the sewing machine, pulling it out from the back. Gently roll the beads a little between your fingers so that the stitching falls between the beads to become almost invisible.

5 Flat ribbon or braid can be fed through a ribbon/braiding foot and stitched in place with a decorative stitch. Use a thread color to contrast, match the trim, or use a clear thread so the stitching is virtually invisible.

Flower attachment

This little gizmo is fantastic! It fits all sorts of sewing machines and can be used to decorate fabric with different-sized circular flowerheads. It is used with the feed dogs lowered and a decorative stitch pattern such as three-step zigzag, blind-hem, tricot, or other stitch-width pattern.

Handy hint
If you don't have two spool holders, wind some thread onto a bobbin and place it on top of the thread reel on your spool holder.

WHAT THE FLOWER ATTACHMENT LOOKS LIKE

The flower attachment has a large circular base with notched steps and an arm that is placed over the needle holder attached to a spring-loaded clip that moves over the steps one by one as the needle goes up and down (see above). To attach it, the presser foot shank is first removed so that the attachment can be fixed directly to the needle holder. On some models it is necessary to have a short shank adaptor too.

A center prong, moved left or right when the retaining screw is loosened, determines the size of the flower stitched. As with any concentrated areas of stitching, it is advisable to sew on two layers of fabric or use interfacing, tearaway, or another stabilizer on the back. This will prevent the fabric from puckering. Try out different stitches and threads on scraps of fabric before committing to a project.

CONCENTRIC STITCH

To stitch concentric circles, set the center prong in the direction of the (+) and sew the outside circle using a three-step zigzag or tricot stitch. Then raise the needle and presser-foot level, loosen the screw on top of the device, and slide both the large disc and the fabric to set the prong in the direction of the (-). Lower the presser foot, tighten the screw, and sew the inside pattern.

TRANSPOSITION STITCH

Stitch one circle and then stitch another one over the top, slightly transposed so that the "petals" of the new circle fall between those of the previous circle. After sewing the first flower circle, raise the presser foot level and click the notched disc forward to the third, sixth, or ninth notch and stitch again around the same circle, the stitches falling either side of those previously made.

USING THE FLOWER ATTACHMENT

1 Lower feed dogs (see User's Manual). Set the needle position to the left and reduce top tension on thread to 3.5–3.

2 Attach foot, with protruding arm hooked over the screw fitting on the right of the needle holder.

3 Bring bobbin thread to top and hold tails behind the work. Select a widthwise stitch such as zigzag, and set to widest stitch width. Sew slowly, taking care not to trap or catch the fabric so that the attachment can turn the fabric smoothly as it stitches. Return needle to left position, stitch a few stitches on spot, and remove work to cut threads.

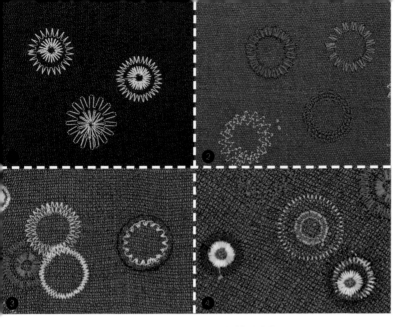

Using a twin needle

Try using a twin needle and playing with different thread colors. Insert the twin needle and thread with two different colors (put one on a spindle to unravel clockwise and the other on a second spindle to unravel anti-clockwise to prevent threads tangling).

Work some flowers with the right side of the fabric facing the throat plate so that it is the bobbin thread that shows.

Checking stitch choice

Twin needles come with different gaps between the needles, so check your stitch choice carefully to ensure both needles clear the flower-stitch attachment and needle throat plate when stitching both left and right swings of needles.

Tightening the screw

Always tighten the screw holding the flower attachment in place with a screwdriver so that it doesn't work loose when you are stitching.

IDEAS FILE

1 Concentric stitch: Smaller flowers stitched off-center in the middle of the large flower can look good too!

2 Transposition stitch: Experiment with widths of stitch to make this overlapping stitch.

3 Combination stitch: Combine concentric circles with transposition stitch to create more variations. Change thread for added variety.

4 Two thread colors: Try using more than one thread color at a time in the twin needle.

4 To change the flower size, realign the center prong with the +/- guide on the front by loosening and tightening the screw at the back of the attachment. The nearer the prong is to the minus sign, the smaller the flower, and vice versa.

5 Use any widthwise stitch, but check that the needle will not hit the side of the attachment or throat plate by turning the balance wheel on your sewing machine by hand for the first few stitches. If the needle looks likely to hit the throat plate, reduce the stitch width and try again.

Husqvarna Viking
chenille foot

Chenille foot

A chenille foot creates a soft, chenille embellishment on fabric. It allows strips of bias-cut fabric to be fed under the needle and stitched to the surface of a separate cloth. With the help of some laundering and distressing, the chenille effect is achieved.

WHAT A CHENILLE FOOT LOOKS LIKE

This snap-on foot has a broad opening at the front to feed bias strips, up to $5/8$in (16mm) wide, through it and under the needle. The strip is held centrally so that the stitching sits in the middle, parallel to the edges, thus giving a neat finish. The chenille foot has a smooth underside to hold the layers flat below it. The wide aperture for the needle allows the needle to swing to each side and take both zigzag and straight stitching.

HOW A CHENILLE FOOT WORKS

Feed between one and eight bias-cut strips of fabric through the guide in the front of the foot and under the needle. With an additional layer of cloth placed below it, stitch the strips in position. When completed, the layers of fabric are washed and distressed to create a soft, fluffy texture on the surface—this is chenille. The more layers of strips used to create the chenille, the denser the effect.

Making chenille without a specialist foot

An alternative method for creating chenille is to sew a series of parallel lines through the layers of fabric, then cut between the lines of stitches to form the strips. The fabric is then washed and fluffed up as before. The difficulty with this method is cutting all the top layers without snipping the backing fabric accidentally.

Before attaching the foot

Try placing the end of the strips into the guide at the front of the foot before attaching the foot to the sewing machine. It can be easier to handle this way rather than feeding the ends into the guide when the foot is already attached to the sewing machine.

SEWING WITH A CHENILLE FOOT

Although chenille can be created with a standard presser foot, this specialist attachment simplifies the process (see box, above right).

1 Attach the chenille foot to the sewing machine by snapping it into place. Thread up the machine with appropriate thread which either blends or contrasts with the fabric, depending on the result required.

2 Select fabrics that will fray easily and cut long, bias strips of fabric measuring $2/3$in (16mm) wide. Choose one color or mix three, four, or more plain and/or printed fabrics, depending on the desired result.

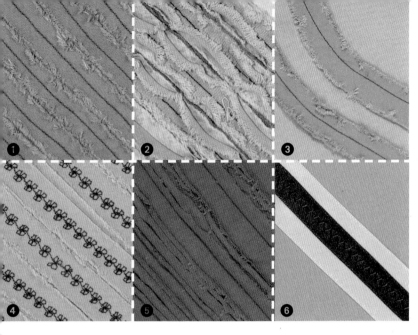

Fabric choices for chenille

To achieve the best results when making a chenille embellishment, choose loose weave materials that fray easily. Fabrics made from 100 percent cotton fiber, including quilter's cottons (plain and printed), denim, and challis work well or select thicker wools and tweeds.

Cutting strips

To achieve the chenille effect, the strips need to be cut on the true cross or bias. The easiest method of cutting bias strips is with a rotary cutter, a patchworker's ruler, and a self-healing mat placed below. Find the true cross (45 degrees) to the grain and cut strips measuring ⅔in (16mm) wide. If a rotary cutter is not available, use long-bladed shears for the smoothest cut.

To manage the depth of layers
Lengthen the stitch and reduce the pressure of the presser foot to manage the depth of layers.

IDEAS FILE

Single strips on a matching backing: Cut bias strips and sew these singly onto a backing of the same fabric.

Three different colored strips sewn to a fourth fabric as a backing: Cut bias strips in three different fabrics and sew to a backing fabric. Choose colors that work well with each other.

Curves: Sew the strips to the backing cloth in curves rather than straight lines for a wave effect.

Decorative stitch: Sew the strips to the main cloth with a decorative stitch as an extra detail. However, as the chenille foot has a flat base with no channel, there is no space for a build-up of stitches, so be sure to choose an uncomplicated decorative stitch.

5 Stretch knit: A stretch knit fabric, like cotton T-shirting, cut in the direction of most stretch rather than on the cross, gives a different effect to traditional chenille. The knit fabric naturally curls to the right side.

6 A guide for stitching ribbon: Use the chenille foot as a ribbon guide, sewing different widths together or sewing them to a fabric. For narrower widths, feed the ribbons directly through the needle slot as it will hold it steady for stitching.

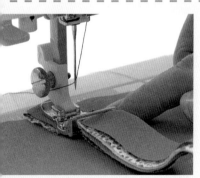

3 Feed one or more bias strips into the guide at the front of the chenille foot. Place the backing fabric (which can either be the same or a contrast color) under the presser foot and lower the foot to hold the layers together.

4 Select a longer than standard straight stitch and sew the strips to the backing fabric. Make several rows parallel and adjacent to each other.

5 Launder the resulting layers of fabric in the washing machine and line or tumble dry. Use a stiff bristled brush to further distress the edges and encourage the soft bloom of the ravelled chenille appearance.

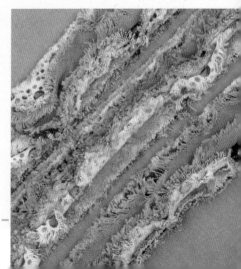

Candlewicking foot

Use this specialist presser foot to recreate the traditional craft of candlewicking with a sewing machine rather than by hand sewing. Originally, a form of white work sewn with thick thread/floss on muslin, a similar effect is possible by programming suitable stitches on a modern sewing machine.

Husqvarna Viking
candlewicking foot

Use curved needlework scissors
Buy a pair of curved needlework scissors to snip away the jump threads between candlewick knots more easily.

WHAT A CANDLEWICKING FOOT LOOKS LIKE
This metal snap-on foot is open at the front with wide access for good visibility. It has a very deep groove on the underside to take the build-up of stitches or knots so that they will pass below the foot unhindered.

HOW THE CANDLEWICKING FOOT WORKS
The traditional use of knots to form the texture of a candlewick design is produced with dense machine stitches to create a similar appearance. These are either already built into the sewing machine when purchased or produced by programming a series of bulky stitches into the memory. The foot allows the stitches to be viewed as they are formed, then pass under the presser foot in the deep channel below.

Stabilizers
A stabilizer is a layer added to support fabric when sewing. It adds body and stiffness so that the stitches are formed properly and do not pull or sink into the fabric. Stabilizers can remain behind the work when completed but they are often removed by tearing, cutting, or washing away. Choose firm stabilizers that properly support the material.

SEWING WITH A CANDLEWICKING FOOT
Create a candlewick effect by machine to embellish all sorts of bags, soft-furnishing projects, and garments.

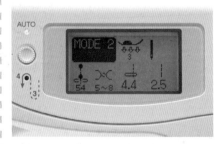

1 Select a suitable knot-like stitch for candlewicking by choosing a built-in stitch or programming one of your own. Snap the foot to the sewing machine.

2 Transfer an appropriate design to the fabric using a wash-away or fade-away temporary marker. Draw the outline or a series of dots to use as a guide when sewing.

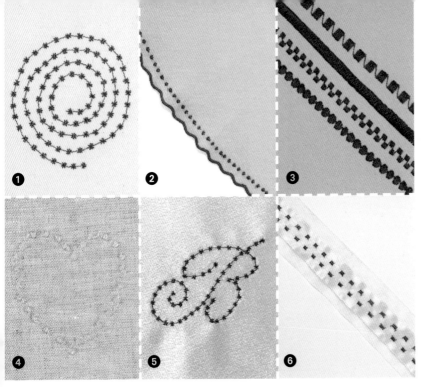

① ② ③

④ ⑤ ⑥

Making candlewick stitches

If your sewing machine does not have specific candlewicking stitches, look for those that have a knot-like design like a series of stars or close satin stitches joined by a number of straight stitches. If you are using an electronic or computerized sewing machine, it is possible to create your own tailor-made stitch. Look at the manual for programming tips.

Candlewicking designs

If you are stuck for suitable candlewicking designs, look in children's coloring books. These are full of simple line drawings that can be adapted for candlewicking.

IDEAS FILE

1 Spirals: Sew spirals of candlewick stitches for a textured design.

2 Border: Create a border on the hem of a skirt or tablecloth with candlewicking stitches matched with other decorative stitches. Here we have sewn a row of large candlewick stitches above a wavy row of satin stitches and trimmed the excess up to the satin stitches.

3 Satin stitches: Use the candlewick foot to sew any bulky decorative stitches as the space below the foot allows these to pass under without being obstructed.

4 White work: The traditional candlewicking effect was created in neutral colors with the emphasis of the design being on texture. Choose a simple motif and sew over the outline with thread of the same color as the backing. An attractive yet subtle effect is formed.

5 Monogramming: Use the candlewicking foot to sew monograms. Draw the outline of the letters in a wash-away or fade-away marker, then sew.

6 Ribbon: Use the candlewicking effect on ribbon or even join two ribbons using off-set candlewicking stitches.

3 Place the fabric under the candlewicking foot and lower the needle into the guide line. When perfectly positioned, lower the presser foot and start to sew.

4 Follow the guide line and complete the whole design in "knot" stitches.

5 The knots may be joined with a long jump thread or several shorter threads. If possible, snip and remove these joining threads to leave only the knots in place.

Janome clear
appliqué foot

Appliqué foot

When creating appliqué with a sewing machine, a dedicated foot makes it easier to see the line being followed to sew the stitch exactly where it is needed. It both supports the fabric around the needle and allows a clearer view of the work.

Use a heat-fusible film for sewing appliqué

A heat-fusible film like Bondaweb or Wonder Under is a great product to use when sewing appliqué. Iron it to the wrong side of the fabric, draw the outline shape on the paper backing, and cut out. Remove the paper, then position the motif on the backing fabric and iron in place. It holds the appliqué motif in position and eliminates the need for basting.

WHAT AN APPLIQUÉ FOOT LOOKS LIKE

The appearance of an appliqué foot varies but generally it is short in length and sometimes open at the front. Often it is made from clear plastic. It has a deep channel on the underside. Some types look very like the open toe foot (see page 78).

HOW AN APPLIQUÉ FOOT WORKS

An appliqué foot is a simple design often with a broad slot for the needle to swing to make a zigzag stitch or completely open at the front for a better view of the stitch area. It is generally clear plastic so that the stitches are visible as they are formed. The deep groove underneath the foot allows the build-up of stitches to pass unhindered and the shorter length makes it more maneuverable for following a particularly intricate design.

SEWING WITH SATIN STITCH AND AN APPLIQUÉ FOOT

The outline of an appliqué design can be sewn with a standard or zigzag foot but the technique is much easier to produce with an appliqué foot.

1 Prepare the appliqué design and secure it to the backing fabric with basting, temporary spray adhesive, or a heat-fusible product (see box, above left).

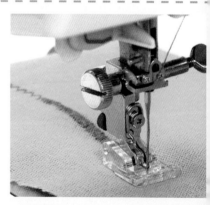

2 Set the sewing machine to zigzag and reduce the length of the stitch to create dense stitches for satin stitching. Alter the width of the stitches to suit the task; a wider stitch gives a bold outline, while a narrow satin stitch is more delicate.

Be aware of the reversed image

When cutting out a design for appliqué, be aware that the image will be reversed when drawing the outline on the wrong side. This is not a problem when the shape is symmetrical but some numbers and letters will be reversed.

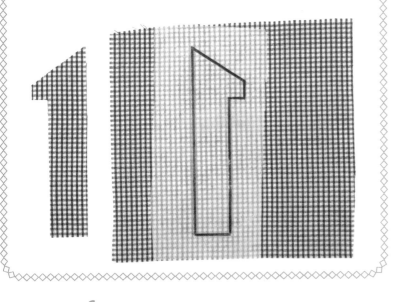

Finding designs for appliqué

When looking for designs to use for appliqué, look in children's coloring books for simple, uncluttered outlines.

Fixing appliqué designs before stitching

There are various methods of securing an appliqué design to a backing fabric before machine stitching.

1 Basting: Position the appliqué design onto the main fabric and baste round the outside to hold it in place. Remove the basting after the machine stitching is completed.

2 Heat-fusible film: Trade names include Bondaweb or Wonder Under. See Tip, left.

3 Temporary spray adhesive: Shake the can well and spray the wrong side of the appliqué motif before placing the design onto the backing fabric. This method will hold the two fabrics together until the machine stitching is complete. Use the spray can outside or in a well-ventilated room.

4 Fusible thread: See step-by-step sequence on page 104 for creating padded appliqué using an appliqué foot.

3 Snap the appliqué foot in place and follow the outline of the appliqué to permanently hold it in place. This will also help to make the design stand out.

4 Pull the thread ends to the wrong side and tie off or thread onto a needle to secure them.

5 Finish the design with additional satin stitching if required.

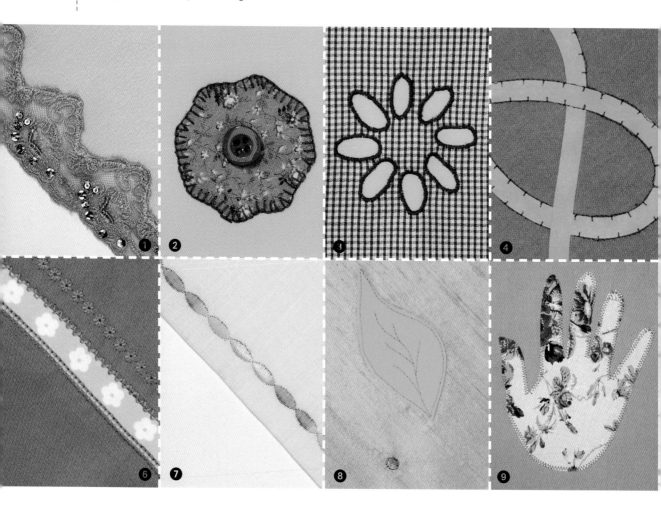

CREATING PADDED APPLIQUÉ USING AN APPLIQUÉ FOOT

A 3-D effect can be created by stuffing an appliqué shape to give extra depth.

1 Wind fusible thread onto the bobbin and place it in the sewing machine.

2 Draw the motif shape on fabric and, with the right side of the fabric facing up, sew on the outline with a straight stitch. Cut away the excess fabric just outside the line of stitching.

IDEAS FILE

1 Attaching lace: Attach shaped edging lace to the hem of a garment with a zigzag stitch and cut away the main fabric behind to retain the sheer nature of the lace.

2 Blanket stitch: Choose a blanket-style stitch to outline appliqué. Set the sewing machine to a pre-programmed stitch and adjust the length and width to suit.

3 Reverse appliqué: Cut away the upper fabric to reveal the areas of the fabric below and neaten the raw edge. Here, a narrow satin stitch has been used in a contrasting color.

4 Bias tapes: Sew bias tapes or ribbons in place with a suitable pre-programmed stitch like this blanket-type stitch. It secures the tape without giving a bold outline. Use invisible thread for an even neater finish.

5 Printed fabric: For appliqué, use designs on printed fabric. Flowers are popular, as are novelty prints for children, such as teddy bears or cars. Cut round the shape and satin stitch them to the background.

6 Attaching ribbons: Use an appliqué foot when stitching ribbons to a backing and embellish with other decorative stitches. Make use of the fancy stitches available in the memory of the sewing machine.

7 Decorative stitching: Use the appliqué foot when adding a decorative line of stitching to a garment or home decorating project. The foot allows the sewer to see exactly where the stitches are being formed.

8 Felt: When felt is cut, a clean edge is created which does not ravel. A simple straight stitch can then be used to hold it securely in place.

9 Zigzag stitch: For a fast finish, select a simple zigzag stitch to hold the appliqué to the backing. Zigzag stitch will be quicker to sew than satin stitch.

10 Intricate designs: When sewing a complicated design, the appliqué foot enables a good view of the sewing line so that it can be followed accurately. Here, a triple stitch, normally for reinforcing or for stretch stitching, is used to form a bolder line.

4 Make a small slit in the backing fabric behind the appliqué design and fill with stuffing. Close the slit with hand sewing when sufficiently padded.

3 Iron the motif to the main fabric. The fusible thread will melt and adhere to the backing fabric to hold it in place. Set the sewing machine to satin stitch, then sew round the outline over the first line of stitching.

5 The completed appliqué is slightly padded, making it more interesting.

Circular sewing attachment

Brother circular
sewing attachment

Janome circular
sewing attachment

Sewing a circle freehand is tricky, but with a circular attachment fixed to the sewing machine, perfect circles can be achieved. These circles can be created using decorative stitches, ribbons, or couched threads, and are a great way to embellish bags, purses, cushions, and bedding.

WHAT A CIRCULAR ATTACHMENT LOOKS LIKE

Circular attachments vary in appearance, depending on the make of sewing machine. However, they all have a central pivot point and an adjustable radius so that different sized rings can be sewn.

To make small circles
For smaller circles, use the flower attachment on page 96.

HOW A CIRCULAR ATTACHMENT WORKS

Once fitted to the sewing machine, fabric is pinned to the central point of the circle. The fabric pivots at this midpoint, so stitching is formed in a ring around it. The radius is adjusted to create the size of the circle required and this means a number of concentric circles can be sewn from the same central point.

To finish a circle
Where the end of the stitching meets the beginning on the circle, leave long thread tails and remove the work carefully from the machine. Thread the tails on to a needle and pull through to the wrong side to finish them securely.

IDEAS FILE

1 Decorative stitches: Select a number of different decorative stitches and sew concentric circles using the same central point.

2 Scalloped edge: Neaten the edge of a circle with a scallop stitch, then trim away the excess fabric to give a pretty outer rim. Sew these to hats or garments, or use as coasters.

3 Couching: Fit a cording foot to the sewing machine and thread decorative cords or pearl cotton through the guides. Set the sewing machine to a three-step zigzag and stitch the cords in a circle to a backing fabric. The zigzag stitch catches all the threads in place. For a neat finish, pull the cords and threads to the wrong side of the fabric to secure them.

4 Ribbons: Use a ribbon foot to guide the ribbon or braid under the needle and, with the help of the circular attachment, sew perfect circles of ribbon.

SEWING WITH A CIRCULAR SEWING ATTACHMENT

Use this foot to embellish fabrics with perfect circles of stitching, ribbon, beads, sequins, or decorative threads.

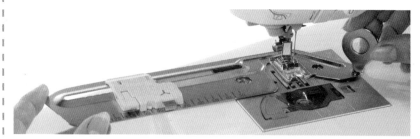

1 Fit the circular sewing attachment to the sewing machine, following the manufacturer's instructions. In addition to the attachment, choose a suitable presser foot, depending on the type of sewing, for example, decorative stitching, ribbon attachment, pearl foot.

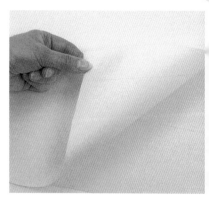

2 Fix a stiff stabilizer to the wrong side of the fabric. Use a temporary spray adhesive and a tear-away stabilizer for best results, as this will hold the work flat but can be removed afterwards.

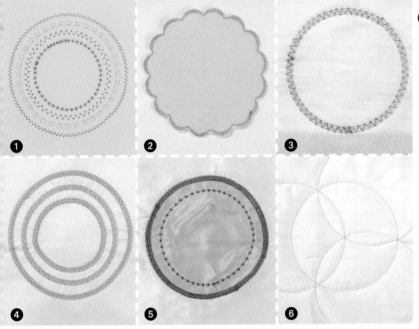

① ② ③

④ ⑤ ⑥

Steady stitching with hoops

Rather than use a firm stabilizer on the wrong side, place the fabric into a hoop to hold it flat and steady for stitching. However, it may be necessary to remove the presser foot from the sewing machine to slip the rim of the hoop under and into place. Make sure a large hoop is used to prevent the needle bar from hitting the edge of the hoop.

In our example here, we have sewn a circle of pearls with a pearl foot and the circular attachment. Snip the excess pearls away and secure with the thread tails threaded on to a needle.

5 Circular appliqué: Cut the appliqué fabric larger than required and place it over the backing fabric. Use a temporary spray adhesive to hold it in position. Sew a straight stitch in the circle through both layers, then trim away the excess fabric of the top layer. Set to a satin stitch and sew over the edge of the circle.

6 Quilting: For perfect quilted rings, use the circular attachment and a straight stitch. Lengthen the stitch and fit a walking foot to cope better with the thick layers and overlap the last few stitches over the first few to secure the thread ends. Move the center of each circle.

To protect the fabric
Place a small piece of stabilizer over the center of the circle where the pin or tack will penetrate the fabric to give extra strength to protect the fabric at this point.

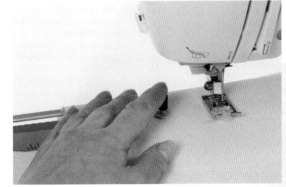

3 Mark the center of the circle with a temporary marker pen and place the circular sewing attachment pin through this point.

4 Slide the fabric under the presser foot and locate the position for the pin to sit in. Push to hold the pin securely at the center of the circle.

5 Select an appropriate stitch and sew, keeping the fabric flat in the process. This ensures that the circle will be perfectly round.

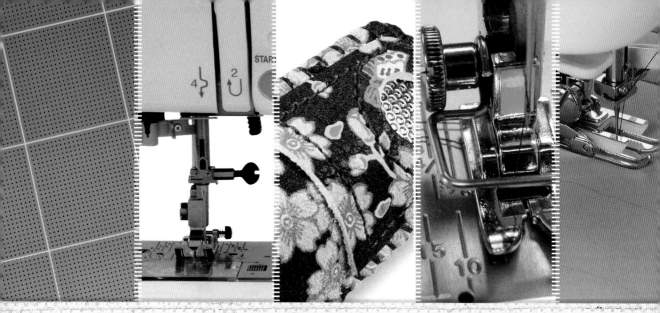

CHAPTER 6

Buyer's guide

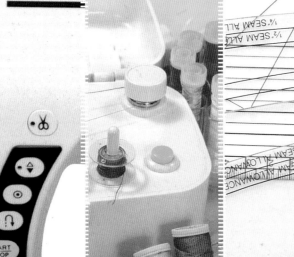

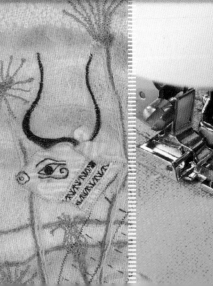

A book about using a sewing machine wouldn't be complete without a look at choosing a new model. Whether you wish to buy a new machine because yours is a hand-me-down, or whether you wish to upgrade, there's advice on basic, mid-range, and top-end machines, as well as specialist models. We start with a buyer's 15-step guide to help you determine the type of machine that will best suit your needs. Under each subsequent category of basic, mid-range, and top-end machines, there's a handy list of typical features so you can make your own checklist of must-haves.

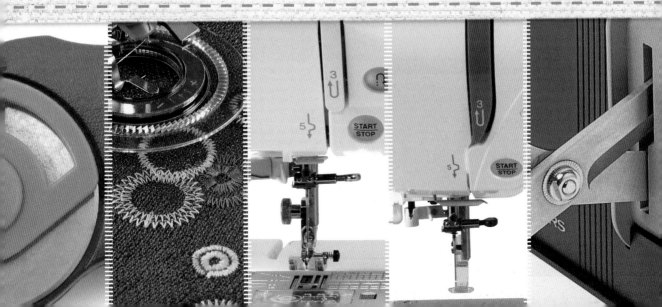

Buyer's 15-step guide

Choosing and buying a new machine should be a pleasure, but it can also be a little daunting because of the enormous choice available. Follow this 15-step guide to simplify the decision and help narrow the choices.

Pin-tuck foot
A pin-tuck foot enables you to create perfect parallel pin-tucks.

1 Are you really only interested in small projects, soft furnishings, or repairs, so want a good basic model? A basic straight and zigzag stitch machine is ideal. However, do check that you can still buy different presser feet to help with more specialist techniques.

2 Will you want to get creative with free-motion embroidery (when you drop the feed dogs and use an embroidery foot)? If so, again, a basic model is perfectly suited as you can create wonderful textural art with them.

3 Will you want to stitch lots of customized items using decorative stitches? Look for a machine with a wide range of in-built designs—it will help you make a simple project look stunning.

4 Do you wish to stitch bulky projects like quilts, drapes, and throws? If so, you will need a robust machine with good space around the needle. Many manufacturers do specialized quilters' machines with a large work surface and quilters' accessories such as specialist feet and guides.

5 Are good buttonholes a must? Select a machine with easy one-step or four-step buttonholing and a choice of buttonhole designs. This is important if you like dressmaking and sew a variety of clothes.

6 Will you wish to monogram or stitch out names to personalize presents? Look for a machine with alphabets/fonts so you can create your own lettering with ease.

7 Do you love embroidered embellishments and do you want to do embroideries and/or get experimental and manipulate them, or even create your own designs on a PC and then stitch them out? Look for a top-of-the-range computerized sewing machine.

8 Do you want a machine to take on sewing courses? If so, then consider weight and size. Some brands have three-quarter size machines that are lightweight to carry, but still pack a punch with features.

Decorative lacing
A good choice of buttonholes will include tiny eyelets, perfect as decoration or for lacing.

Free-motion stitching
Free-motion stitching highlights areas of a printed fabric.

Flower attachment
Use a universal flower attachment to decorate fabric with pretty circular floral patterns.

9 Try different utility stitches. Try sewing a buttonhole to see how easy it is; try a blind hem, overcast, gathering, and satin stitch. All these stitches are basic stitches that should be easy to do at the turn of a dial or touch of a button.

10 Decide on your budget. Sewing machines are priced from as little as under $150 to over $7,500. Obviously, the higher the price, the more computerized and specialist a machine will be. However, that doesn't mean it's only for expert sewers. Some computerized machines are perfect for beginners because they do so much for you (see page 114).

11 Remember to consider the future too. Choose a machine that does more than you want at the moment so you can grow into it.

12 Nowadays, most modern machines can cope with different fabrics and multilayers. However, if you like to sew on a variety of fabric types, take your own fabric samples and try them out. Many retailers will show you a machine stitching on a stable cotton such as calico, but it is useful to see how it stitches on silks, satin, or thick fleece and denim.

13 Get advice from people you know. Some will love a particular brand for its sturdiness, lightness, number of stitch choices, ease of inserting bobbins, etc. Decide which of these preferences are most important to you.

14 Look for a good after-sales service and an extended warranty as part of the price. Some brands offer three or even five years' parts and labor guarantees. Look into courses or workshops to learn more about your machine.

15 Whenever possible, the best advice is to try before you buy. Have a go on a range of sewing machines to see which you are most comfortable with.

Circular sewing attachment
This attachment will help you stitch in perfect circles.

Zipper foot
A zipper foot has many uses, apart from inserting zippers, including edge stitch, or adding piping or trims.

Basic machines

These are great for beginners and occasional sewers, and as second machines for courses/workshops.

These simple sewing machines are affordable and sturdy workhorses. They are ideal to take on courses as they are fairly lightweight, and have a carrying handle and protective case. Accessories are stored in an attached compartment (which forms part of the flatbed of the machine).

The downside is that you have to adjust stitch lengths and widths yourself, so there is an element of trial and error in the stitch performance (though the sewing machine manual should provide guidance on the correct settings for different stitch techniques). You may also have to adjust tensions, although for most general sewing, the standard tension, shown by the highlighted number on the dial, is perfectly acceptable on modern machines.

As you go up in price in the basic category, machines come with a small LCD screen in which you will see the recommended foot needed for the stitch selected, the stitch length and width, and a mono image of the stitch formation. Stitch selection is also usually by button rather than dial.

MUST-HAVE FEATURES
- Look for easy threading and easy stitch selection.
- Check out the feet offered — they should include straight stitch, zipper foot, buttonhole foot, overcast foot, and possibly a blind hem foot.
- Check whether the needle position can be changed and the presser foot pressure altered.
- Check the warranty terms.

Avoid adjusting the tension
Avoid adjusting the tension unless absolutely necessary. Modern machines stitch well on all sorts of fabrics quite easily. Any adjustments should be made gradually.

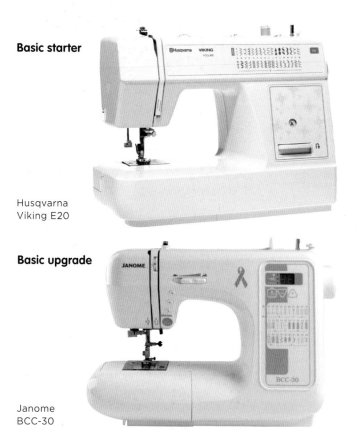

Basic starter

Husqvarna Viking E20

Basic upgrade

Janome BCC-30

Typical features: basic starter
- A limited selection of in-built stitches that are selected by turning dials on the front of the machine.
- Stitch length and width dials that will be included in all but the very cheapest machines (so you have control over the length and width of stitches, which is useful when sewing very lightweight or bulky fabrics).
- An automatic buttonhole—either four-step or one-step.
- The facility to convert to a free arm in order to stitch small areas such as sleeves.
- Drop the feed dogs option for free-motion stitching.
- Auto needle threading.
- Self-lubrication.

Typical features: basic upgrade
- Lock/fix stitch buttons.
- A slide speed control so you can control how fast the machine stitches.
- The reverse stitch button, which may be more conveniently situated just above the needle.
- The presser foot pressure dial which allows you to alter the pressure of the foot—useful when sewing very lightweight or very thick layers of fabric.
- More needle positions are available. Use the stitch width dial to move the needle to the right, left, or center when stitching with a straight stitch.

Mid-range machines

Mid-range machines are ideal for general sewers who like to experiment a little, and who enjoy some decorative and individualization such as adding monograms or names.

These include electronic and simple computerized models—ideal for general sewing, from dressmaking and quilting to crafts and soft furnishings. They are also called entry-level computerized machines. They will have all the features of a basic model, plus much more.

As these models increase in price, so do the specifications and features offered. The number of built-in stitches goes up, often into the hundreds, there are several choices of buttonholes, more fonts for lettering, and more memories for storing your own stitch patterns.

Typical features: mid-range starter

- The LCD screen shows stitch selection, presser foot, recommended stitch length and width.
- They have some automation, including setting optimum stitch width and length for the selected stitch, and automatic tensions (all of which can be altered if you prefer to change them).
- A greater selection of in-built stitches.
- Some have a memory function so you can create stitch combinations and store them for later use.
- Stitch selection, and stitch width and length are easier to change, using buttons rather than dials, which can be awkward.
- Many have a knee-lift, which is a shaped metal rod that fits into the front of the machine and is used to raise and lower the presser foot by pushing against it with the knee. It means you don't have to take your hands from the work.
- Presser foot pressure adjustment so you can increase or decrease the pressure on the foot to suit either very lightweight or heavy, thick fabrics.

Typical features: mid-range upgrade

- Auto lock/fix stitch allows stitching to be automatically fixed by the push of a button so you don't have to tie off thread ends or work them into the back of the work.
- Auto thread cutter means that not only are the stitches locked by stitching on the spot automatically, threads are taken to the back and thread ends cut.
- With needle up or down, you can choose whether the needle remains down when you stop, or always finishes up. This is very useful when constantly stopping to pivot work, such as appliqué or intricate stitched areas.
- Mirror-imaging stitch patterns: turn patterns 180 degrees—useful when creating new customized stitches or matching borders on right and left, or top and bottom of a project.
- Frequently used utility/basic stitches may have an easy one-button selection option.
- Machines aimed at quilters will also have specialist ¼in (6mm) foot, a walking foot, and extra high presser foot lift to enable you to feed in and stitch bulky layers of fabric.

MUST-HAVE FEATURES

- Large selection of built-in stitches.
- Memory function so your own stitch combinations can be saved.
- Clear LCD screen showing presser foot required, stitch choice, length, width and tension.
- Auto lock stitch.
- Easy one-step buttonholes.
- Good selection of basic feet, including zigzag/satin stitch foot, buttonhole, blind hem, overcast zipper, and button sewing foot.
- Needle position options so you can position the needle just where you want it.
- Wider sideways stitch patterns to create more intricate and interesting decorative stitching.
- Seven-piece feed dogs for greater control on feeding fabrics smoothly.

Bernina B350 PE

Mid-range starter

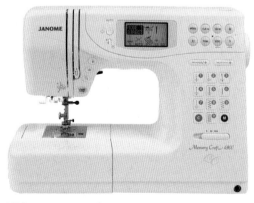

Mid-range upgrade   Janome MC4900 QC

Top-end machines

This group would probably be on every sewer's wish list of sewing machines as they really are super machines that do virtually everything except make the tea! They are computerized and may include embroidery units with the ability to stitch an infinite number of embroidery designs and patterns. They are also great for basic sewing as they make it so easy. Once a stitch is chosen, the machine sets the right tension, stitch width and length, and recommends the right foot and needle size.

On the embroidery side, top-end machines have an impressive number of designs to choose from, the option to buy additional designs via the internet or on embroidery cards, or even expand into designing your own embroideries with PC design software. They can also stitch at incredibly fast speeds of approximately 1,000 stitches per minute, which is useful when stitching complex embroideries. However, they are big and heavy, and therefore not easy to move about, and do require considerable space, particularly when used for embroidery.

Staying with the positives, apart from the obvious features such as the huge choice of in-built stitch designs, embroidery patterns, and alphabets, and all the advantages of the mid-range machines like the auto lock/fix stitch, auto cut, auto threading, etc., these models will also have the following plus points.

■ **Lighting:** Most top-end sewing machines have multiple lights so that even dark fabrics can be seen easily. On some models you can adjust the lighting from cool to warm to suit the time of day and the fabric being sewn.

■ **Wide sewing space:** Some models are geared to quilting so have a very large sewing area between the needle and the side of the machine. This is particularly useful if you sew bulky projects, from coats and jackets, to curtains and quilts.

■ **Ease of converting to embroidery machine:** Most of these machines will have a separate embroidery unit that you attach when you wish to stitch out embroideries. They are big, particularly those that can be used with mega-size hoops, which is great for stitching wonderful large designs, but they are heavy and do take up a lot of room. Janome's top model has the embroidery unit built in and converts to embroidery at the touch of a button, while other models have a separate embroidery unit. Again, when fitted, you can switch from embroidery to sewing at the touch of a button. Space availability is an important consideration here.

■ **Look out for powerful on-board editing:** You can then cut, copy, paste, flip, rotate, zoom in, and see the layout in 3-D before stitching the pattern. Check whether the machine you are considering can convert embroidery files to the format needed— many do.

■ **Connecting to your PC:** Check whether you can connect directly to a PC to download new designs both from the internet, and those you have created using appropriate software. Some manufacturers also enable you to upgrade your machine via the internet.

Quilting
Top of the range machines make short work of time-consuming tasks like quilting. Shown here is the walking foot in action.

Typical features

- A large, color touch screen for easy stitch/ embroidery selection and manipulation. It also shows all the information needed about stitch choice, what it looks like, stitch width, length, foot to use, needle choice, tension, etc. When embroidering, it will show the design, moving the cursor as the design is stitched out.
- A stop/start button so you can sew without using a foot pedal. The button is sited just above the needle so it is easy to reach without taking your hands from the work.
- A sewing adviser or help menu advice on how to sew different techniques, or what stitch and foot to use for different fabric weights.
- The facility to alter stitches to create your own patterns. These include mirror imaging, repeat, moving the position of an embroidery, combining embroidery designs, and much more. They also have memory facilities so you can store your newly created stitch pattern for future use.
- Options to input more designs using embroidery discs or cards, or by linking directly to a PC. Here, the options continue to expand, as with the right software you can create your own embroidery designs on a PC, adding color, stitch patterns, etc., then transfer them to the sewing machine to stitch out while you take a break!

MUST-HAVE FEATURES

- Check that the machine comes with some tuition. Most do. With machines that have so much to offer, it's important that you can go back to the dealer for tuition and help once you have had a good play yourself.
- Write down all the features that are important to you, whether it's a large sewing space for bulky projects, easy connection to PC and creative design facilities, perfect general sewing, or even the amount of room it will take up when set up. Also, decorative stitch width might be important; some models have the widest stitch width at ⅙ in (6 mm), while others go as high as ⅓ in (9 mm).
- Check whether you can "read" and stitch out embroidery designs from other sources without having to convert them to your model of machine.
- Consider the price of optional extras and those that you might feel are must-have features.
- Consider whether you will want to be able to upgrade your machine and whether it is possible to do so via the internet.

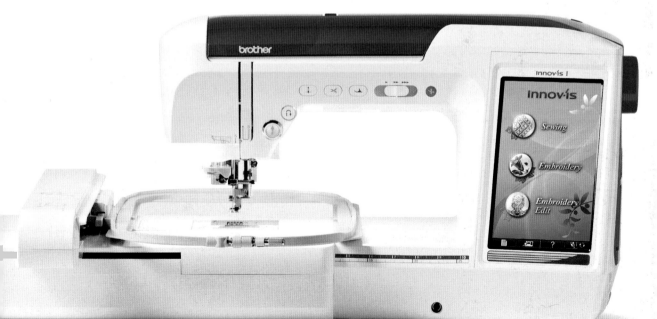

Brother Innovis One

Specialist machines

We now turn our attention to specialist machines that are dedicated to a particular type of sewing. In this category, we have included embroidery-only machines, embellishers, and sergers.

Buy two different machines
If space is limited and weight and price a consideration, consider buying an embroidery machine and a separate sewing machine to cover both types of sewing.

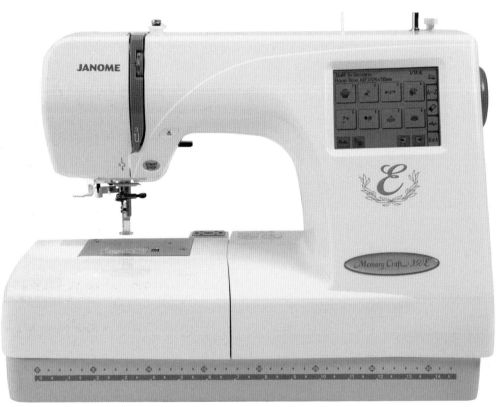

Embroidery-only
An embroidery-only machine such as this Janome model is reasonably priced and provides the chance to stitch wonderful embroidered designs similar to those created by top-end embroidery/sewing machines.

Janome MC350 E

EMBROIDERY-ONLY MACHINES

These machines are designed to stitch out embroideries only and cannot be used for general straight stitching and dressmaking. Thus they are smaller, lighter, and considerably cheaper than the top-of-the-range sewing and embroidery machines. It's a less expensive way to upgrade to embroidery capability.

Of course, as with the top-of-the-range machines, these models include lots of in-built embroidery designs, as well as the option to add more via embroidery cards or USB sticks as most of them will also allow you to transfer designs you have created on a PC with design software. Most will have on-board editing facilities so designs can be combined, decreased, or increased in size.

Look for a model with an auto thread cutter, which is a real boon when stitching out multicolor designs with lots of color changes. The machine will fix the stitches, take the threads to the back of the work, and cut them. There may be a limitation to the maximum hoop size you can use. The backlit LCD screen is smaller than the top-of-the-range machines and may be a mono screen.

Use a long-arm quilting service
If you don't want or need to go to the expense of a long-arm quilt machine, you can use a long arm quilting service to baste the layers of your quilt together before hand- or machine quilting.

Pfaff QE4.0

Quilting machine

Ensure a permanent fix
Felt from the top, from the reverse of the work, and again from the top to ensure a permanent fix.

Janome FM725

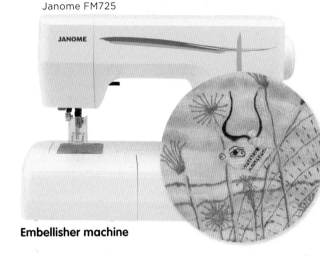

Embellisher machine

QUILTING MACHINES

Quilting machines include specialist features that suit working with bulky projects, such as a large extension table to cope with vast, flat quilts, a bigger workspace between the needle and side of the machine, as well as specialist feet—walking foot, quarter inch, and stitch in the ditch foot. Some have a stitch regulator, so even if you are free-motion quilting, the stitch length is evenly spaced automatically.

LONG-ARM QUILTING MACHINE

The long-arm quilting machine is designed to sew decorative patterns on large areas using a straight stitch. This stitches all the quilting layers together with no need for pinning and basting. It incorporates a large table, tracks that move the needle head from one end of the quilt to the other, and an integrated system to hold and roll the quilt not being worked on. Stitch designs can be customized. These machines vary in size, price, and features, but all models require a large space for the table, rollers, and tracks.

Most of the new long-arm quilting machines are computerized, offering more choices in stitch design. This means you can ensure accurate pattern and block size, control the number of stitches per inch, any desired repetitions of the pattern, and the offset of the pattern. These machines work at high speeds and are multidirectional, so typically require stronger thread than a regular home-sewing machine,

therefore, use threads with a high tensile strength such as polyester, cotton-wrapped polyester core, and pure cottons.

EMBELLISHER MACHINE

It looks like a sewing machine, but it isn't. It is a needle felting machine, with a set of barbed needles that punch through fabric layers, catching fibers on the barbs and meshing them together. Depending on the make and model, an embellisher will have a set of three, five, or even 12 needles grouped in a holder that go up and down as you press the foot pedal. However, there is no thread involved, no tension, bobbin, or stitching. Beneath the throat plate is a space to gather the fluff that forms from the meshing.

In some machines the needles can be replaced individually if they break, in others they come as a unit. Unlike sewing-machine needles, they can last for extended periods and you don't need to change them when they become blunt as they are supposed to snag the fabric.

The embellisher is used to create textural fabrics by needle felting two or more layers together. It works well with most natural fibers, wools, felt, silks, and satins. You can also effectively texturize single layers of fabrics, such as organza or silk. Ideal materials to use are felt, felting wools, wool tops, natural fibers, or long-haired fiber. The more you work an area, the more the fibers are pushed to the back and will remain securely in place.

Sergers

While an embellisher looks like a sewing machine but isn't, a serger (or overlocker) looks very different, but does sew seams like a sewing machine. It also trims the seam allowance and neatens the edges, all in one pass. This saves considerable time and produces a very neat finish.

A standard serger has one or two needles as well as two loopers which sit in the body of the machine in place of the bobbin of a sewing machine. These use three or four cones of thread to construct and neaten seams. By selecting the cones of thread to sew with and adjusting the tension of each thread, different stitches can be achieved, such as rolled hem or flatlocking.

More modern and sophisticated models use additional threads and have more needles and loopers enabling other stitches to be sewn including chain stitch and cover stitch.

Sergers use a lot of thread, particularly in the loopers, so are often threaded with a lightweight, fine thread that is cheap and less bulky. Soft woolly threads are often used in the loopers, creating a softer feel when worn against the skin. Thread tends to come on cones.

Most have differential feed which means they will feed both layers of fabric together evenly and stitch a nice flat seam without rippling and puckering. There is usually a choice of three settings: 0.7 for lightweight fabric, normal (center) for average-weight fabrics, and 2 for stretch fabrics which are selected using a dial on the right-hand side (sometimes a window on the front of the machine shows the selected number).

Stitch length is changed by another dial on the side (again there may be a window showing the selection on the front of the machine). Generally, the smaller the number, the smaller the stitch, thus use lower numbers for lightweight fabrics and higher for heavy fabrics.

SERGER STITCHES
Most sergers will sew a range of different stitches for seaming and hemming, including three-thread, four-thread, rolled hem, lettuce edge, and flatlocking.

> **Practice threading your serger**
> Practice threading your serger so that you are confident that you can do so easily. It is the threading that often puts people off using these wonderful machines.

Typical features
- Most sergers have two needles with the option of using both (for very secure stitching), removing the left (for narrow stitching) or the right (for wider stitching). Some have a third needle which sews chain stitch. **(1)**
- At least two loopers sit in the body of the machine below the needles in place of the bobbin or spool of a sewing machine. As these have a hole rather than an eye, thicker threads can be used to give decorative effects. **(2)**
- There are two blades which cut the fabric ready to be covered and neatened with overlock stitches. The lower blade remains stationary, while the upper blade moves to cut the fabric just before it is stitched. The upper blade can be de-selected so that you do not cut the fabric edge at all, for instance, when making pin tucks. **(3)**
- Most machines have tension dials to control the thread as it passes through the guides to the needles and loopers. This enables different stitches to be created, such as balanced overlocking, rolled hemming, and flatlocking. **(4)**
- The stitch dial controls the distance the stitches sit from each other. They can be very close, as on a rolled hem, or further apart like on a picot edge. **(5)**
- The differential feed enables the fabrics to pass under the presser foot evenly without being constrained or stretched. This can be used to prevent stretching or even to encourage it to achieve a particular effect, such as lettuce edging, which forms a curly hem by deliberately putting more threads and stitches into the edge than necessary. **(6)**

Cones and cops
Serger threads come on cones or cops and are often a finer thread.

MUST-HAVE FEATURES

- Easy threading—some sergers are easier to thread than others. Generally, the more expensive models have features making them easier to thread and use.

- Two-thread option—most standard sergers use three and four threads to form the stitches. An additional two-thread option gives a delicate rolled edge and a better flatlock stitch.

- Free arm option—some models have a removable section to allow sleeves or hems to be slipped over the arm of the machine making cuffs and hems easier to sew.

- Cover stitch machines—some sergers also enable a cover stitch to be produced. This appears like two parallel lines on the right sight side of the fabric and is used for hemming manufactured garments. It is necessary if clothing is to appear store-bought rather than homemade.

Threading a serger

Threading a serger can be daunting, particularly the loopers. The easiest method is to cut thread ends of those already on the machine and tie on the new threads, pulling them through until they get to the needles before cutting off the knots and threading manually. If this is not possible, follow the diagram, usually found on the flip-open front cover of the machine. It.is often necessary to thread the machine in a certain sequence, lower looper, upper looper, then needles. Check your user's manual to confirm, as failure to thread in the right sequence can result in the machine not looping/stitching correctly.

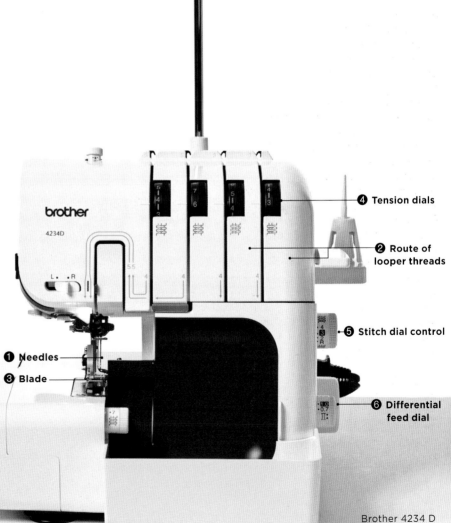

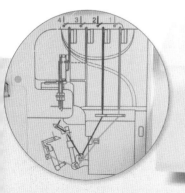

4 Tension dials

2 Route of looper threads

5 Stitch dial control

6 Differential feed dial

1 Needles

3 Blade

Brother 4234 D

Troubleshooting

No matter how careful you are when using your sewing machine, it is inevitable that there will be occasional problems. The troubleshooting guide below should help in most circumstances, but don't forget the value of the sewing machine manual for the specifics of your own model.

PROBLEM	POSSIBLE CAUSES	REMEDY
Will not sew	Power not reaching machine.	Check power is on and all plugs and flexes are connected fully.
	Some machines have safety mechanisms which prevent them from operating if doors or flaps are left open.	Ensure all doors and flaps are shut.
Breaking needles	Needle not inserted fully; it is bent so hits presser foot; too fine for the fabric being sewn or is not clamped tightly enough.	Refit or replace with a suitable needle and clamp securely.
	Stitch and presser foot not suited and needle hits foot when sewing—for example, zigzag stitch with a straight stitch foot attached.	Change stitch or foot as necessary.
	Build-up of threads under the fabric in the machine breaks the needle as it tries to sew.	Remove bobbin and threads, defluff, then reinsert bobbin in race.
	Wrong bobbin or spool (possibly from a different make or model) has been inserted into the race or bobbin holder.	Ensure correct bobbin is used.
	Upper thread is too tight and is pulling on the eye of the needle.	Cut and rethread the machine, ensuring it runs smoothly before continuing to sew.

SEWING MACHINE

PROBLEM	POSSIBLE CAUSES	REMEDY
Uneven stitches	Presser foot and/or feed dogs not feeding fabric evenly.	Make sure the feed dogs are operating (switch on if necessary) or increase the pressure of the presser foot so that it progresses the fabric steadily and consistently.
	Sewing over a bulky seam—for example, hem of jeans.	Use a humper jumper gadget (see page 17).
	Decorative stitches unevenly spaced can be caused by using the wrong presser foot—for example, one with a smooth base.	Use a suitable presser foot with a deep groove in the base to slide over the build-up of stitches (open toe, zigzag, appliqué, or candlewicking).
Skipped/missing stitches	Needle is bent or blunt.	Replace the needle.
	Upper threading may be incorrect.	Cut and rethread ensuring it runs smoothly.
	Thread and needle combination may be wrong.	Select a more suitable needle for the thread choice or type of fabric.
	Needle incorrectly threaded.	Rethread correctly—from front to back in most cases, and occasionally left to right.

STITCHES

	PROBLEM	POSSIBLE CAUSES	REMEDY
STITCHES	Puckered stitches/fabric	Disappointing decorative stitches or machine embroidery pulling on the backing fabric can be caused by lack of support beneath the fabric.	Place a suitable weight of stabilizer on the wrong side of the fabric or add another layer if using one already.
	Loose needle stitches	Loose upper stitches may be caused by incorrect threading, different top and bottom thread, or poor tension.	Check that the thread in the reel and bobbin are the same, then rethread the sewing machine (upper thread and bobbin). Only increase needle tension slightly if nothing else helps.
	Loose bobbin stitches	Loopy threads below are likely to be due to poor threading, different top and bottom thread, or poor tension.	Check that the thread in the reel and bobbin are the same, then rethread the sewing machine (upper thread and bobbin). If the tension has not improved, loosen the needle tension slightly. Do not adjust the bobbin tension, but seek advice from an engineer.
FABRICS	Stretching seams and hems	If the wrong foot is fitted, fabrics can be permanently stretched making hems and seams ripple.	Fit a walking foot or roller foot to feed the fabric evenly and prevent it from stretching too much.
	Stitches too visible on a blind hem	When blind hemming, choosing an appropriate color of thread is important so the stitches are hidden.	Select an appropriate thread color (a shade darker is best). Increase the stitch length so that stitches are farther apart.
		Too much stitch is seen on the right side.	Carefully adjust the blind hem foot to ensure the needle just catches the fold as it swings to the left. The chosen fabric might be too thin for a successful blind hem as it works best on medium- and thicker-weight cloth.

PROBLEM	POSSIBLE CAUSES	REMEDY
Fabric puckers or pulls	If fabric pulls tight, it could be the result of poor tension or pulled threads from the needle or bobbin.	Rethread the sewing machine and also remove and replace the bobbin in the bobbin holder. If the puckering is minimal or on a lightweight fabric, apply slight pressure to the fabric behind the presser foot to ease its progress while sewing. If this does not help, adjust the needle tension slightly.
Disappearing fabric	The fabric may be pushed down into the machine below the feed dogs, jamming the mechanism. This can damage the machine as well as the fabric. This can be caused by too thick a needle for the weight of fabric.	Fit a size 10/70 needle.
	Very fine lightweight fabrics get pulled into the feed dog gaps.	For straight stitching, fit a straight stitch foot and needle plate to give more support around the needle. For other stitching, choose a foot with more support closer to the needle.
Fabric not progressing	Feed dogs may be lowered or pressure on the foot may not be sufficient.	Check feed dogs are raised or increase the pressure of the presser foot.
Fabric layers not being fed evenly	The pile on the fabrics rub and feed unevenly.	Sew seams with a walking foot or roller foot. Alternatively, reduce the pressure of the presser foot.

FABRICS

Glossary

Appliqué
Motif or additional fabric attached to the surface of the base cloth.

Basting (tacking)
Temporary stitching by hand or by machine.

Bias
Diagonal direction of fabric between the warp and the weft threads.

Bias binding
Fabric strip that is cut on the bias and folded in half to be wrapped around raw seam edges to encase them.

Bobbin fill
Extremely fine thread used in the bobbin when sewing machine-embroidered designs.

Cutting line
Commercial patterns have a bold outer line, which is the cutting line. Sometimes a seam line is also shown. If not, generally seam allowances are ⅝in (1.5cm) on dressmaking patterns.

Ease
Designers add ease to dressmaking patterns to provide ease of movement and style. There can be wearing ease and designer ease within a garment.

Ease stitch
Used to fit a slightly longer piece of fabric onto a shorter length, ease stitch is sewn just within the seam allowance with a slightly longer stitch length. Often used to insert set-in sleeves into an armhole.

Edge stitching
Type of topstitching visible on the outside of a garment, but usually stitched a scant ⅛in (3mm) from the edge.

Fabric
Result of yarns having been woven or knitted together. In some cases, fibers are felted or bonded direct into fabric.

Feed dogs
These teeth lie under the presser foot and protrude through the throat plate. They move the fabric to allow the needle to make each stitch.

Fiber
Refers to a single natural or synthetic "hair," which is then spun with others into a yarn.

Finger pressing
When using an iron is not appropriate, fingers can push fabric into place.

Free-motion stitching
Creative stitching when the feed dogs are lowered and thus you can move the fabric in any direction as you stitch.

Gimping
Also known as "couching," gimping is used to describe stitching down yarns laid on the surface of a fabric.

Interfacing
Stabilizing fabric placed onto the wrong side of a dress fabric to add support to an area—for example, a collar or pocket.

Mercerization
Treatment applied to cotton to give it strength and luster.

Muslin
Test or mock-up of a garment made in a cheap cloth. In the U.K., this is referred to as a "toile."

Nap
Surface texture on a cloth which makes it appear different from different angles. Pattern pieces must be cut in the same direction on a napped fabric.

Notions
Items required to complete a garment or project, including zippers, buttons, elastic, etc.

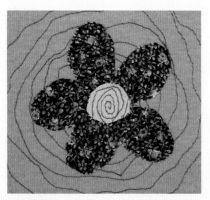
Appliqué

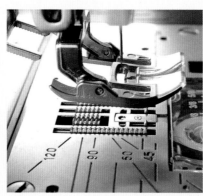
Feed dogs

Gimping

Overcasting
Zigzag or other wide stitching sewn over a raw edge (or edges) to neaten and prevent fraying.

Pile
Extra fibers or loops which have been woven or knitted into a fabric during manufacture—for example, on velvet or toweling.

Pilling
Through wear, small balls of fiber appear on the surface of some synthetic fabrics. They can be picked or cut off. Also known as bobbling.

Quilting
Stitches sewn to hold fabric layers together and either made by hand or sewing machine.

Satin stitch
Very close zigzag stitch used to cover raw edges of appliqués or to create letters. The smaller the stitch length, the closer the stitches are together.

Seam allowance
Distance between the stitching line and the edge of the fabric when sewing pieces together. A standard ⅝in (1.5cm) is often used.

Selvage/selvedge
Finished side edges of a cloth which do not ravel.

Sew-through button
Button with two or four holes, through which you sew to attach a button to a garment.

Shank button
Shaped button with a loop on the underside through which you sew to attach a button to a garment. The raised loop ensures there is space between the button and the fabric so that when bulky fabric is buttoned it will lie flat.

spi
Stitches per inch. An alternative to using millimeters to describe stitch length.

Stabilizer
Bonded fabric which is used to support fabric being sewn with decorative stitching or embroidery, and is normally cut away or removed afterward.

Stay stitching
Straight stitch used to hold fabric stable and prevent it from stretching. Usually stitched just within the seam allowance.

Stitch in the ditch
Pieces are held together by stitching on the right side of a previously made seam—for example, on a waistband.

Topstitching
Stitching that is purposefully visible on the surface. Often used to add detail or simply to hold facings etc. in place.

Under stitch
Seam allowances are stitched to the facings only and the stitching is not seen on the right side—for example, on pants side pockets, neck facings, etc.

Warp
Threads are put on the loom first before a fabric is woven. The weft threads are then woven between from left to right.

Weft
Threads making up the filling yarns of a woven cloth.

Without nap
Fabric without a napped surface does not need to have all its pattern pieces cut in the same direction, as there is no surface shading or texture.

Satin stitch

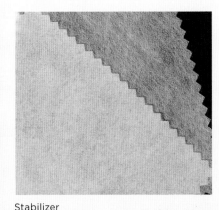

Stabilizer

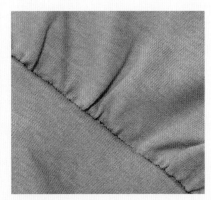

Stitch in the ditch

Index

Credits

With thanks to Janome sewing machines for the loan of one of their lovely computerized models for our step-by-step sequences, and to Bernina, Brother, Elna, Husqvarna Viking, and Pfaff for the use of their sewing machines, feet, and attachments. Thanks also to Lez Gardiner and Phil Langford for additional photography.

All photographs and illustrations are the copyright of Quarto Publishing plc. While every effort has been made to credit contributors, Quarto would like to apologize should there have been any omissions or errors—and would be pleased to make the appropriate correction for future editions of the book.